Commentaries on CANADIAN LITERATURE

CELEBRATING
LITERATURE & CULTURE

Commentaries on CANADIAN LITERATURE

S. RAMASWAMY

Prestige

an international publishing house

Published by
Prestige Books
3/28, East Patel Nagar
New Delhi 110 008
Mobile: 9818755529

ISBN: 81-7551-173-7

Rs. 500
Prestige Books
International

Printed at Chaman Offset Press, New Delhi 110 002

Contents

POETRY

DRAMA

FICTION

GENERAL

Foreword

The present volume contains twenty-two papers presented by me at the International Conferences of the Indian Association for Canadian Studies over the years where, as a Life Member, I have been presenting papers regularly. Six of the papers included here have been published—one in the *International Journal of Canadian Studies* (Ottawa) two in *Indian Journal of Canadian Studies*. Twelve had not been published so far. The papers in the volume cover various aspects of Canadian Literature. Some of them about Canada and India—ranging from general considerations like regional literature of the Prairie and French Canada to significant individual poets like Margaret Atwood and Anne Hebert, dramatists like Sadhu Binning and Rana Bose, fiction writers like Elise Aylen and Rohinton Mistry. While there are essays on women-Canadian dramatists like Beverley Simon, Erika Ritter and Sharon Pollock, there are essays on the Indian diaspora dramatists like Sadhu Binning and Rana Bose. The essay on "Canadian Bi-Culturalism" talks about the 'Two cultures'—the Anglophone and the Francophone—discusses the bilingualism of Canada. Thus the papers cut across the various regions of Canada as well as the different genres like Poetry, Drama, Fiction and general topics like Environmental Changes, Humour and Satire, Immigration and Globalization and Women's writing. The title *Commentaries on Canadian Literature* has been used to establish a continuity with the two earlier volumes of mine published by Prestige Books in 1994 entitled *Commentaries on Commonwealth Poetry and Drama* and *Commentaries on Commonwealth Fiction*. It is hoped that the present volume will also find a similar reception where also there are a number of essays on Canadian Literature. I am grateful to Prestige Books, especially Dr. R.K. Dhawan, who has published this volume also.

Engendering Gender
Margaret Atwood's *Murder in the Dark*

> It is subversive of me even to write these words.
>
> Margaret Atwood

> But just because all rapists are men it doesn't follow that all men are rapists, you tell yourself . . . How can you like men? . . . Still, you continue to believe it can be done. If not all men, at least some, at least two, at least one. It takes an act, of faith.
>
> Margaret Atwood

Margaret Atwood's *Murder in the Dark* is a curious literary document which is described as her 'seventh work of fiction or tenth work of poetry' depending on how we see it. These pieces can be read as prose poems, as fictionalized autobiography, as parables, as mini romance or as mini science fiction. However, the present paper doesn't concern itself with the form of this entertaining, experimental and unusual work of the author. It concerns itself with engendering gender as it is dealt with in a light-hearted bantering tone which reveals Atwood's humour at its best. One would expect such a sense of humour from a Mark Twain or Stephen Leacock but it comes as a total surprise in a writer like Margaret Atwood. What is attempted in the following lines is not a critical analysis of either the work under consideration or of the nature and quality of her humour. The idea is to just present her 'Prose Poems' as they are to partake of the enjoyment the present writer has experienced in reading them.

The subversive attitude is revealed when she parodies things which are treated seriously. For example the description of a strip-tease act:

> One woman began with her back to the audience, the spotlight on her. She was wearing long white gloves and a black evening down with gauzy black sleeves that looked like membranous wings as she stretched out her arms. She did a lot with her arms and back; but when she finally turned around, she was old. Her face was powdered dead white, her mouth was a bright reddish purple, but she was old. I could feel shame washing through me, it was no longer funny, I didn't want this woman to take off her clothes. (15)

Every aspect of sex is made fun of. Take the following narration

> A ship's master has disappeared. He was seen entering a whorehouse but he was not seen coming out. This man has to check out all the whorehouses in town, to find the right one. If the ship's master can't be located, dead or alive, the widow gets a million dollars, which naturally the ship-owners would rather not pay unless they have to.
>
> Isn't it dangerous? I say.
>
> A whorehouse is the safest place around, he says. They have a reputation to keep up. I always get a policeman to go with me. (19)

Atwood is facetiously funny which is a part of her subversive narrative technique. The piece entitled *Murder in the Dark* from which the book itself takes its title is another illustration of her tone of voice:

> This is a game I've played only twice. The first time I was in Grade Five, I played it in a cellar, the cellar of a large house belonging to the parents of a girl called Louise. There was a pool table in the cellar but none of us knew anything about pool. There was also a player piano. After a while we got tired of running the punchcard rolls through the player piano and watching the keys go up and down by themselves, like something in a late move just before you see the dead person. I was in love with a boy called Bill, who was in love with Louise. The other boy, whose name I can't remember, was in love with me. Nobody knew who Louise was in love with. . . . So we turned out the lights in the cellar and played 'Murder in the Dark' which gave the boys the pleasure of being able to put their hands around the girls' necks and gave the girls the pleasure of screaming. . . .

> The second time I played it was with adults; it was not as much fun, though more intellectually complex. (29)

Atwood doesn't spare women novelists either though she is herself one. The light-hearted comments sometimes go deeper and the light-heartedness is only a facade to reveal a serious insight. In her piece entitled 'Women's Novels' she says:

> Men's novels are about men. Women's novels are about men too but from a different point of view. You can have men's novel with no women in it except possibly the landlady or the horse, but you can't have a women's novel with no men in it. Sometimes men put women in men's novels but they leave out some of the parts—the heads, for instance, or the hands. Women's novels leave out parts of the men as well. . . .
>
> Men favour heroes who are tough and hard: tough with men, hard with women. Sometimes the hero goes soft on a woman but this is always a mistake. Women do not favour heroines who are tough and hard. Instead they have to be tough and soft . . .
>
> Men's novels are about how to get power. Killing and so on, or winning and so on. So are women's novels, though the method is different. In men's novels, getting the woman or women goes along with getting the power. It's a perk, not a means. In women's novels you get the power by getting the man. The man is the power. But sex won't do, he has to love you. (34-35)

This is a typical passage which reminds one of the witticisms of another writer of 'Prose-Poems,' Charles Baudelaire, the famous French writer whose *Intimate Journals* contain many such comments. For example he says: "What is annoying about love is that it is a crime in which one cannot do without an accomplice!" Following this piece there is another called 'Happy Endings' where Atwood discusses half seriously and half jocularly the art of writing. She suggests many endings for the same novel, which covers the entire gamut of possible ways in which the novel can proceed to its logical or illogical denouement. It has all to do with answering the question which she raises at the beginning of the discussion: "John and Mary meet. What happens next?" Actually, any number of things. She suggests six "happy endings"! The first ending called 'A' runs this way:

> John and Mary fall in love and get married. They both have worthwhile and remunerative jobs which they find stimulating and challenging. They buy a charming house. Real estate values go up. Eventually, when they can afford live-in help, they have two children, to whom they are devoted. The children turn out well. John and Mary have a stimulating and challenging sex life and worthwhile friends. They go on fun vacations together. They retire. They both have hobbies which they find stimulating and challenging. Eventually they die. This is the end of the story. (37)

After four more alternatives we get to a fifth which is an interesting variation which recollects ironically the above ending with a difference.

> If you think this is all too bourgeois, make John a revolutionary and Mary a counter-espionage agent and see how far that gets you. Remember, this is Canada. You'll still end up with A, though in between you may get a lustful brawling saga of passionate involvement, a chronicle of our times, sort of. (40)

We end up with

> The only authentic ending is the one provided here: John and Mary die. John and Mary die. John and Mary die. (40)

There is no form of literature that Atwood does not look at with an amused insight. For example there is a comment on the 'fairy tale':

> There were once two sisters. One was rich and had no children, the other had five children and was a widow, so poor that she no longer had any food left. She went to her sister and asked her for a mouthful of bread. 'My children are dying,' she said. The rich sister said, 'I do not have enough for myself,' and drove her away from the door. Then the husband of the rich sister came home and wanted to cut himself a piece of bread; but when he made the first cut, out flowed red blood.
>
> Everyone knew what that meant.
>
> This is a traditional German fairy-tale. (42)

Here Atwood is making a comment on the heavy German moralizing even if it is in the form of an allegorical 'traditional German fairy-tale.'

The man-woman relationship—engendering gender—which is the central theme of *Murder in the Dark* is revealed even in titles of some of these 'Prose Poems.' For example, 'The Boy's Own Annual,' 'Boyfriends,' 'Women's Novels,' 'She,' 'Him,' and 'Liking Men.' About liking men, she says:

> It's time to like men again. Where shall we begin? I have a personal preference for the backs of necks, because of the word nape, so lightly furred; which is different from the word scruff. But for most of us, especially the beginners, it's best to start with the feet and work up. To begin with the head and all it contains would be too suddenly painful. Then there's the navel, birth dimple, where we fell from the stem, something we have in common; you could look at it and say. He also is mortal. But it may be too close for comfort to those belts and zippers which cause you such distress, and comfort is what you want. He's a carnivore, you're a vegetarian. That's what you have to get over. (53)

It is in the same piece that she says: 'Just because all rapists are men it doesn't follow that all men are rapists,' which has been quoted as the motto at the beginning of this essay. At this point a brief reference may be made to her short story *Rape Fantasies*. The story takes a look at 'female space' from a very unusual angle. A traumatic subject is dealt with in a dramatic but light-hearted tone. The story is an ironic contemplation with wit, sarcasm, genial humour and even an element of parody. The would-be rapists—there are eight of them—turn out to be not only harmless but downright pathetic creatures, one or two of them such romantic and chivalrous gentlemen who need to be reminded of their intentions! The final quotation from the present work, *Murder in the Dark*, which is in the form of a quasi-serious comment on the art of the writer is entitled 'Instructions for the Third Eye':

> The eye is the organ of vision, and the third eye is no exception to that. Open it and it sees, close it and it doesn't.
>
> What's the difference between vision and a vision? The former relates to something it's assumed you've seen, the latter to something it's assumed you haven't. Language is not always dependable either.
>
> Try not to resist the third eye; it knows what it's doing. Leave it alone and it will show you that this truth is not the only truth. One day you will wake up and everything, the stones by the driveway, the brick houses, each brick, each leaf of each tree, your own body, will be glowing from within, lit up, so bright you can hardly look. You will reach out in any direction and you will touch the light itself. (61-62)

This 'inside comment' by Atwood on the art of a writer also reveals her comic vision in this most unusual work of hers.

We started by saying that Atwood's *Murder in the Dark* is a curious book. The form that she has chosen to put in her thoughts just as they come without apparently any conscious design or order is responsible for transforming realism into surrealism, fancy into fantasy. Giving free reign to her association of ideas and stream of consciousness gives her an objectivity where the writer of a controversial work like *Survival* chooses to talk about surviving tactics in a totally comic context which would perhaps shock ardent, deadly serious, committed feminists. The mode of presenting this idea in this essay has been not so much to present a systematic paper but to share the sheer enjoyment that the present writer has experienced in reading this extraordinary document by one of the major Canadian writers. Beneath all the light bantering fun, there is a serious comment on the art of fiction itself of which Atwood herself is an excellent example. This is the reason why we talked of the idea of subversion which defines this whole work.

NOTE

1. Margaret Atwood, *Murder in the Dark: Short Fictions and Prose Poems* (Toronto: Coach House Press, 1983).

The Poetry of Anne Hebert

I believe in the virtue of poetry. I believe in the salvation of all right words lived and expressed. I believe in solitude broken like bread by poetry.

Anne Hebert, *Poesie, Solitude Rompue*

Anne Hebert was one of the first modern poets that I read—in any language—and her work made an indelible impression on me. I still know some of her poems virtually by heart—they both capture and create their own world.

Margaret Atwood

Anne Hebert who has been hailed as a major world poet and Canada's most important French poet of the twentieth century has also created her own 'poetic' in her essays like *Mystere de la Parole* (The Mystery of the Word), *Poesie, Solitude Rompue* (Poetry: Solitude Broken). It is best to begin with her own statement:

> Poetry is a profound and mysterious experience which we attempt in vain to explain, to locate, to seize at its source and in its own interior progress. It begins bound with the poet's life and grows out of his substance like his flesh and blood. It calls from the bottom of his heart like another life, reclaiming its right to the word in the light. And that singular adventure which begins in darkness, at the sacred point of life that presses and forces the heart, is called poetry.[1]

A fact that is very often neglected is that Canada is a bilingual country. It is good to remember at the very outset:

> Canadian literature may be divided into two parts, somewhat like a tree with two great roots. One root is deeply buried in the culture of France. The other is just as deeply buried in the traditions of England. One part of the Canadian literature is written in French,

> the other in English. But the branches of this tree are firmly Canadian. Authors and readers of each literature are gaining more and more knowledge of the other in the original or in translation.[2]

The same idea is emphasized in a figurative manner by Robertson Davies, who in his lecture on "The Canada of Myth and Reality" says:

> Two stereotype figures have arisen from the pressures of our political situation; one is a wistful, large-eyed, pitiful girl in the peasant dress of the eighteenth century, and the other is a coarse-grained, large-footed, evil-visaged Scotch banker, to whom she is bound in a hateful marriage from which she seeks to escape. The mismated pair is, of course, Quebec, La Belle Province, and the other parts of Canada.[3]

The reason for discussing Anne Hebert here is to draw attention to the fact that Canadian writing in French has not received the attention that it richly deserves, even in English translation. At this stage it may be interesting to remember a poem about Canadian poets and poetry by F.R. Scott:

The Canadian Authors Meet

Expansive puppets percolate self-unction
Beneath a portrait of the Prince of Wales.
Miss Crotchet's muse has somehow failed to function,
Yet she's a poetess. Beaming, she sails

From group to chattering group, with such a dear
Victorian saintliness, as is her fashion,
Greeting the other unknowns with a cheer—
Virgins of sixty who still write of passion.

The air is heavy with 'Canadian' topics.
And Carman, Lampman, Roberts, Campbell, Scott
Are measured for their faith and philanthropies,
Their zeal for God and King, their earnest thought.

The cakes are sweet, but sweeter is the feeling
That one is mixing with the literati;
It warms the old and melts the most congealing.

Really, it is a most delightful party.

Shall we go round the mulberry bush, or shall
We gather at the river, or shall we
Appoint a poet laureate this Fall,
Or shall we have another cup of tea?

O Canada, O Canada, Oh ca
A day go by without new authors springing
To paint the native maple, and to plan
More way to set the selsame welkin ringing?[4]

Apart from the poets that are mentioned here Carman, Lampman, Roberts, Campbell, Scott, the recent Anglophone poets like E.J. Pratt, Earle Birney, Malcolm Lowry, A.M. Klein, Irving Layton, P.K. Page, Margaret Atwood, Margaret Avison are familiar names. However, French poets like Octave Cremazie, Louis Frechette, Lucien Rainier, Albert Lozeau, Emile Nelligan, Rene Chopin, Simone Routier, Francois Hertel, Saint-Denys-Garneau are less familiar. Hebert herself is perhaps the most Quebecois poet who has naturally been translated into English along with a number of other Quebec writers. Her major works are *Les Songes en equilibre* (Montreal: Editions de l'Arbre, 1942), *Le Tombeau des Rois* (Quebec: Institut Litteraire du Quebec, 1953), *Poemes* (Paris: Editions du Seuil, 1960), *The Tomb of Kings* (trans. Peter Miller, Toronto: Contact Press, 1967), *Poems by Anne Hebert* (trans. Alan Brown, Don Mills, Ontario: Musson Books, 1975).

II

The title poem of the collection by the same name *Le Tombeau Des Rois* (The Tomb of Kings) written in 1953 has been described as a classic of modern Quebecois literature:

***Le Tombeau Des Rois* (The Tomb of Kings)**

My heart's on my fist
Like a blind falcon.

This taciturn bird gripping my fingers

Lamp swollen with wine and blood,
I go down
Toward the tomb of kings
Amazed
Barely born.

What Ariadne's thread leads me
Through the muffled labyrinths?
Echoes of footsteps swallow themselves.

(In what dream
Was this child's ankle bound
Like a spell-bound slave?)

The author of the dream
Pulls the thread
And naked steps start coming
One by one
Like the first drops of rain
At the bottom of wells.

The smell already stirs in swollen storms,
Oozes under the doorsills
Into the round and secret rooms
Where the walled-in beds are raised.

The dead's torpid desire tugs at me.
Astonished I watch
The blue encrusted stones
Shining among black bones.

A few patiently wrought tragedies
On the breasts of reclining kings
Are offered to me
Like jewels
Without regret or tears.

In one straight line:
The smoke of incense, dried rice-cakes,
And my trembling flesh:
Humble and ritual offerings.

A gold mask on my absent face,

Violet flowers for my eyes,
The shadow of live, precise little lines of my make-up.
And this bird that I have
Breathes
And complains strangely.

A long shiver
Like the wind catching from tree to tree
Stirs seven great ebony Pharaohs
In their solemn decorated cases.

Only the depth of death persists,
Simulating the final agony
Seeking its appeasement
And its eternity
In a thin clash of bracelets,
Vain circles of foreign games
Around the sacrificed flesh.

Avid for the fraternal source of evil in me,
They lay me down and drink me:
Seven times I feel the grip of bones,
The dry hand hunting my heart to break it.

Livid and satiated with foul dreams,
My limbs freed
And the dead thrown out of me, assassinated,
What reflection of dawn wanders in here?
Why does this bird shiver
And turn toward dawn
Its gouged eyes? (61-65)

As *The Oxford Companion to Canadian Literature* points out: "It is an exploration of the unconscious filled with symbols; a bird (the poet), Kings (the voices of the past), jewels and flowers (the allurements of the dead), water (dread), closed chambers (tombs), bones (death), and light (an awakening). Here the liberation is as much psychological as poetic."[5] The present writer does not know of any other poem where images beget fresh images except in W.B. Yeats's *Byzantium.* A few lines from

Hebert's poem "I am Earth and Water" can be quoted here to relate her poetry with her 'poetic':

Je Suis La Terre Et Leau (I am Earth and Water)

> Je suis la terre et l'eau, tu ne me passaras pas a gue, mon ami, mon ami
> Jesuis le puits et la soif, tu ne me traverseras pas sans peril, mon ami, mon ami
> Je suis sans nom ni visage certain; lieu d'accueil et chambre d'ombre, piste de songe et lieu d'origine, mon ami, mon ami.
> (92)
> I am earth and water, you won't wade through me, my friend, my friend.
> I am the well and thirst, you won't cross me without danger, my friend, my friend.
> I have no specific name or face, no resting place or shaded room, path for dreams or birthplace, my friend, my friend. (93)

This poem is almost an illustration of her theory of poetry as she uninitiates it in her essay "Poetry: Solitude Broken":

> Poetry colors beings, objects, landscapes and sensations with a kind of new, particular light which is the poet's emotion. It transplants reality into another living ground which is the poet's heart, and that becomes another reality, as true as the first. The truth that was scattered in the world takes on a distinct and precise face, that of a singular incarnation. (69)

Anne Hebert is a passionate writer and the emotion takes precedence over the intellect. She employs to the fullest extent poetic devices like imagery, symbolism and suggestion. This is so evident in her writing that even her novels are poems in prose. Anne Hebert's themes are: the awakening of the senses, the rejection of the outside world resulting in the retirement into an interior world which represents purity and innocence as contrasted with the outside world which represents evil and solitude. Love, hate and violence are involved in the quest for the authentic self. The blood imagery which predominates her writing is very evident even in her novels *Kamouraska*, *Le Temps Sauvage,* and her tale

Le Torrent which remind one of the writing of the Spanish poet Fredirico Garcia Lorca, whether he is writing poetry or drama. Just in order to stress the point that Canada is a bilingual country and the poetry is written in both English and French, one curious poem which mixes English and French in an amusing manner is given below.

Montreal

O city metropole, isle riverain!
Your ancient pavages and sainted routes
Traverse my spirit's conjured avenues!
Splendor erablic of your promenades
Foliates there, and there your masonry
Of pendent balcon and escalier'd march,
Unique midst English habitat,
Is vivid Normandy!

Grand port of navigations, multiple
The lexicons uncargo'd at your quays,
Sonant though strange to me; but chiefest, I,
Auditor of your music, cherish the
Joined double-melodied vocabulaire
Where English vocable and roll Ecossic,
Mollified by the parle of French
Bilinguefact your air![6]

III

The special appeal of Anne Hebert's poetic to the present writer is the fact that it is very similar to the Indian concept of the word connected with 'Sphota Vada.' The text that is of special interest in the present context is Bhartrihari's *Vakyapadiya*[7] from which Raja Rao derives his two essays on 'The Word.' The poetic of Anne Hebert in *The Mystery of the Word and Poetry: Solitude Broken* abounds in statements like: "Poetry can't be explained; it is lived. It is and it satisfies. It takes its place as a living creature and can be encountered only face to face, in original silence." (71) And "Silence, nothing stirs, nothing's said, the word makes itself, lifts our hearts, seizes the world in a single stormy gesture and glues us to dawn like a peel to its fruit" (79). In Hebert's *Mystere de la Parole* (The Mystery of the Word) she says:

> Silence, ni ne bouge, ni ne dit, la parole se fonde, souleve notre coeur, saisit le monde en un seul geste d'orage, nous colle a son aurore comme l'ecorce a son fruit.
> Toute la terre vivace, la foret a notre droite, la ville profounde a notre gauche, en plein centre du verbe nous avancons a la pointe du monde. (78)
> (Silence, nothing stirs, nothing's said, the word makes itself, lifts our hearts, seizes the world in a single stormy gesture and glues us to dawn like a peel to its fruit.)
> The whole earth alive, the forest on our fith, the dense city on our left, right in the middle of the word, we walk to the edge of the world. (79)

The idea of poetry that it works more at the level of the subconscious and the unconscious and not merely at the conscious level and what is left unsaid, unheard is not only more melodious but the essence of the poem itself. No wonder Eliot felt "Great poetry communicates itself before it is understood." Our concept of the Word has four stages—Para, Pashyanti, Madhyama, and Vaikari. The Word heard belongs to the fourth level. The other three submerged levels speak through 'Silence' in Anne Hebert's terminology and becomes "Mantra" in the words of Raja Rao. In Raja Rao's two essays on the Word "The Writer and the Word"[8] (originally published in *The Literary Criterion*, 1965) and "The Ultimate Word,"[9] he invokes Bhartrihari. He also talks about this Sphotavada—"Sabdatattva"—in his novel *Comrade Kirillov*. It is worth quoting as Raja Rao gives an exact prescription of the theory of the Word according to Indian poetics which is parallelled in a way in Anne Hebert's *Mystere de la Parole* (The Mystery of the Word). The character in Raja Rao's novel explains:

> The word consists of many atomic components—called Sphota. . . . The word principle is conceived as having four stages, Para,

> Pashyanti, Madhyama and Vaikari. The first is beyond comprehension; the second is attainable only by yogis; the third Madhyama is the Sukshma only to one's innate powers of hearing; the fourth is the word as we have it in use. Now it is the third among these that is accepted as the Sphota above enunciated.
>
> The word reduced to its sound value, then to its vibratory value, then finally to its etheric (Akashic is the Sanskrit word for it) structural value, is reduced to exact nothingness. It is this universal nothingness that makes all permutations possible. In modern language we would say all objects are ultimately reducible to the electromagnetic field and sound and object being one, they can be interpreted in terms of the wave equivalents, etc. . . .
>
> A set of human, vocal vibrations—and in this case teleprinted probably—only produce the required physico-chemical transformation of the auditive and cerebral mechanisms, and produce a recognizable sound effect. Then the word is born.[10]

Just one of the definitions given by Bhartrihari of Sphota may be mentioned here:

> Sphotarupavibhagena dhvanergrahanamishyate |
> Kaschiddhvaninirasamvedyah swatantrornaihiprakalpitah ||
> (Certain theorists maintain that reception of the sound takes place without any separation of it from the form of the Word (sphota); others hold that the sound is not perceptible. According to yet others it is an independent manifesting agent).[11]

To give an idea of the mystique and the mystery of Hebert's poetry, one short complete poem entitled "Night" is given here:

> Night
> The silence of the night
> Engulfs me
> Like vast underwater currents.
>
> I rest at the bottom of mute and sea-green water.
> I hear my heart
> Flashing on and off
> Like a lighthouse.
>
> Pulsing rhythm
> Secret code

I can't decipher any mystery.

With each flash of light
I close my eyes
To continue this night
Perpetuate this silence
Where I'm shipwrecked. (25)

To conclude this brief sketch of the poetry of Anne Hebert, the translator of her poems into English, A. Poulin, Jr., may be quoted:

> Anne Hebert is also generally recognized as French Canada's greatest living novelist whose books include *Kamouraska* (1972), *Children of the Black Sabbath* (1977), *Heloise* (1982), and *In the Shadow of the Wind* (1983). She has been the recipient of virtually every major literary award in Canada, including the Prix France-Canada (1958), Prix de la Province du Quebec (1959), Governor General's Award (for poetry, 1961; for fiction, 1975), Prix Malson du Conseil des Arts au Canada (1967) and the prestigious Prix David from the Province of Quebec for the whole of her work (1978). Moreover, she has been the recipient of several major awards in France, including the Prix des Libraries (1971), the Grand Prix du Roman from l'Academie francaise (1976) and Le Prix Femina (1982). In 1982 she was also nominated for the Prix Goncourt in France for *In the Shadow of the Wind.* Meanwhile, there is no doubt in the minds of many that Hebert is a natural candidate for the Nobel Prize for Literature. (154)

NOTES

1. *Anne Hebert: Selected Poems*, trans. A. Poulin, Jr. Stoddart (1988), p. 69.
2. *The World Book Encyclopaedia* (Field Enterprises Educational Corporation, 1975), vol. III.
3. Robertson Davies, "The Canada of Myth and Reality," *Canadian Literature in the 70s* (Toronto: Holt, Rinehart and Winston, 1980), p. 2.

4. *The Oxford Book of Canadian Verse in English and French*, Chosen and with an introduction by A.J.M. Smith (Toronto: Oxford University Press, 1960), p. 188.
5. *The Oxford Companion to Canadian Literature*, ed. William Toye (Toronto: Oxford University Press, 1983), p. 342.
6. *The Oxford Book of Canadian Verse in English and French*, pp. 260-61.
7. Bhartrihari, *The Vakyapadiya*, Cantos I and II with English trans. K. Raghavan Pillai (Motilal Banarasidass, Delhi, 1971), pp. 104-5.
8. Raja Rao, "The Writer and the Word," *The Literary Criterion*, Vol. VII, No. 1, Winter 1965.
9. Raja Rao, "The Ultimate Word," Keynote Address to South Asian Languages Analysis, Round Table Conference at the University of Texas at Austin, 1984. The present writer is grateful to Raja Rao for not only giving him a copy of this but for also encouraging him to explore the concept of 'the Word' in Sanskrit, which he did in the SALA Conference at Cornell University in 1987.
10. Raja Rao, *Comrade Kirillov* (Orient Paperbacks, 1976).
11. Bhartrihari, *The Vakyapadiya*.

Time, Space and Place in Two Canadian Poems: An Indian View

(Kalosmi Lokakshaya krithpravruddaha)
I am come as Time.[1]

(Disashcha Akasashasya aupadhika bheda) Space that is ordinarily spoken as Desa and Akasha are only due to upadhi.[2]

(Mayakalpitha desa kala kalana vaichitriya chitrikrutam)
Space and Time are but the concoctions of Maya.[3]

But now
That the forests are cut down, the rivers charted,
Where can you turn, where can you travel? Unless
Through the desperate wilderness behind your eyes
So full of falls and glooms and desolations,
Disasters I have glimpsed but few would dream of
You seek new Easts![4]

Yes, the Canadian poets have come far from going "round the mulberry bush" and "painting the native maple" and have sought the "new Easts"—and the air is no longer "heavy with Canadian topics"[5] alone. Though all these have surfaced from time to time, naturally, they have survived all this and have transcended into "Eastern" perceptions of Space and Time. As Margaret Atwood has said:

History
is over, we take place
in a season, an individual
space.[6]

Space and Time have always occupied a central consciousness in poets—more precisely, the spacio-temporal transcendence has. Bliss Carman suddenly asks:

> Was it a year or lives ago
> We took the grass in our hands,
> And caught the summer flying low
> Over the waving meadow lands,
> And held it there between our hands?[7]

Carman belonged to that group of remarkable poets which included the Ontario poets Archibald Lampman, Wilfred Campbell and Duncan Campbell Scott. As A.J.M. Smith has pointed out: "These men were all classically educated."[8] In fact, the liberal classical education extended to include an Eastern classical language like Sanskrit. Talking about Cremazie, "the father of French Canadian poetry," Smith says: "He was a man of wide culture. . . . He was well read in English and French, and like some later poets he studied Sanskrit." (xxxi)

Margaret Atwood is not only a central figure in Canadian literature but also "a popular Canadian icon."[9] Some of her poems reveal a remarkable resemblance to Indian philosophical perceptions of Space-Time and empirical reality. The purpose of the present note is certainly not to indicate or imply any Indian or Sanskrit "influences" in the poems of Carman and Atwood but merely to make a cursory comment on two poems from the point of view of how they strike an Indian reader. However, a theoretical foundation is necessary to discuss the concepts of Time and Space briefly in the comparative perspective to see the difference between "Western" and "Indian" metaphysical thinking.

Time and Change in Henri Bergson, Serial Time in Dunne, Time in Existentialism, according to Heidegger, "unreality of Time" in McTaggart and Bradley, Time and Zeno's paradoxes are well known as documents dealing with the concept of Time in Western thinking. Time and the Theory of Relativity in the Western context is not quite acceptable in the Indian metaphysical context. As D.S. Subbaramaiya, a profound scholar in both Physics and Metaphysics, observes:

> Time is conceived of as extending from infinite past to infinite future. There is also the feeling of the lapse of time given expression

> to as 'the flow of time' etc. This concept of time, too, is fairly complex. Here also, the use of numbers on the part of the scientist is of no avail as far as the question of what constitutes time is concerned. Again, it is not decided as to whether time is the totality of instants or a continuum. The concept of the flow of time is not rendered clearer. The involvement of the notion of change in the passage of time does not make it any the clearer, the two concepts being reciprocally dependent. The idea that the notion of events involving the question of 'where' and 'when' together is to be regarded as fundamental in the spirit of the Theory of Relativity which speaks of the space-time manifold, instead of treating space and time as distinct manifolds, adds little towards the clarification of the situation. The notions of 'time-dilatation,' 'relativity of simultaneity,' the measured 'time-interval' being dependent on the motion of the observer etc., raise the question as to whether there is anything like an absolute or universal time at all. The Quantum theory, with its Uncertainty Principle pertaining to energy and time makes it impossible to talk of the precise value of the energy of a system at a definite instant. The principle of continuous increase of entropy brought in to account for 'irreversibility' in nature raises the question as to whether time as such, without relation to bodies and their motions, has any meaning at all.[10]

Archie J. Bahm in his book, *Metaphysics*, discussing the concepts of Time and Space, says:

> The problem of time is difficult to deal with, partly because it is really several problems. Some that will be considered here include; events and duration; how long is the present? simultaneity; levels of time; does the past exist? can there be eternity without time? instantaneity. . . . Space exists. Existence is spatial. What is space? Answers range all the way from "nothing" ("nonbeing," Parmenides) to "everything," or at least "everything physical" (Descartes, "matter" = "extension").[11]

The Indian view of Time and Space can be set forth here to compare—or rather to contrast it—with the Western view. In Indian thinking, Time is denoted by various experiences like *Idanim* "now," *Tadanim* "then," *Kshipra* "soon," *Cira* "later," *Vilamba* "delay," *Yugapat* "simultaneous," *Purva, Agre, Pura* "earlier, anterior," *Pashchat* "later, posterior," *Yuva* "young," *Vriddha* "old," *Kshana* "instant," *Bhuta, Vartamana, Bhavishyat* "past, present, future," *Chalana* "motion," *Parinama* "process of transformation" etc.

The concept of Space takes into account various experiences such as *Iha* "here," *Amutra* "there," *Samipe* "near," *Doore* "farther" *Vyavadhana* "separation," *Parimana* "size," *Dik* "direction," such as East, West, North, South, *Desa* "space," *Pradesa* "place," etc.

The Indian concepts of Space, Time and Place are so different from the western way of thinking that it may not be inappropriate to quote T.S. Eliot on this matter at the risk of sounding chauvinistic:

> Two years spent in the study of Sanskrit under Charles Lenman and a year in the mazes of Patanjali's metaphysics under the guidance of James Woods, left me in a state of enlightened mystification. A good half of the effort of understanding what the Indian philosophers were after—and their subtleties make most of the great European philosophers look like schoolboys—lay in trying to erase from my mind all the categories and kinds of distinction common to European philosophy from the time of the Greeks. My previous and concomitant study of European philosophy was hardly better than obstacle. And I came to the conclusion—seeing also that the "influence" of Brahmin and Buddhist thought upon Europe, as in Schopenhauer, Hartmann and Deussen had largely been through romantic misunderstanding—that my only hope of really penetrating to the heart of that mystery would lie in forgetting how to think and feel as an American or European, which for practical as well as sentimental reasons, I did not wish to do.[12]

However, it is necessary to remember that unlike the Canadian poets, Bliss Carman and Margaret Atwood, Eliot came directly under the influence of Hindu thought and Sanskrit. Consequently his notions of Space, Time and Place show a clear knowledge of Indian philosophical thought. It is significant that Eliot's own doctoral dissertation was on F.H. Bradley. Bradley is the one Western philosopher who comes very close to Shankaracharya in his thinking. Again, Ralph Waldo Emerson, the American transcendentalist shows the knowledge of the *Upanishads*, the *Bhagavadgita* and *Vishnupurana* in his poems like *Brahma*. Archie J. Bahm, talking about the comparative perspective of Western and Indian philosophical thought, says:

> Plato, who influenced the Christian doctrine of time, postulated an eternal realm of pure and perfect ideas or forms that served as patterns used by the creator (demiurgos) in making men and things in the world. "Time is the moving image of eternity." Particular things behave temporally and imperfectly because the eternal forms are only imperfectly embodied in them.
>
> The Neo-Platonist philosopher Plotinus conceived ultimate reality as The One, utterly unrelated to the temporal universe that emanates from it. Levels of being emanating from The One degenerate from a highest level of being without parts, spatial or temporal, through the physical world's levels of increasing plurality of both spatial and temporal parts, toward a beingless void. Events, the shorter the less real, nevertheless do not lack reality, as with Shankara, but exist as less real than the nontemporal and as dependently real. (58-59)

There are many schools of Indian philosophical thought and the present writer is primarily concerned with the Advaita thought as propounded by Adi Shankara. However, it is interesting to quote Archie J. Bahm regarding what he says about Sankhya-Yoga system of Indian philosophy:

> Sankhya-Yoga philosophers divide ultimate reality into two completely different kinds of beings: First, purusha, pure timeless spirits; and, second, prakriti, evolving nature, which like Plotinus' creation devolves from quiescent duration through several stages of increasing activity and differentiation, both spatial and temporal. The minutest flick of action embodies prakriti in its most degenerate form. Accidental encounters between spaceless and timeless spirits and prakriti both lure it from quiescence into activity and create in the spirits a reflected illusion of existing actively and temporally. Yogic liberation of spirits from nature restores them to their nontemporal purity and returns nature to its quiescent state.

> Such quiescence is perfect, hence without events, except that the tendency toward action is perpetually present and is kept in check only by maintaining equalized tensions between the gunas, or forces existing as tendencies to act.
>
> The temporary coincidence of timeless spirits and evolving prakriti (which enjoys an illusion of being conscious in the presence of spirits) in no way influences the nature of either. Neither depends on the other for its nature, although prakriti cannot activate its temporal processes, and thus events, except in the presence of spirits. (59-60)

Regarding the notion of "Place," though the sense of place generally includes the idea of a whole atmosphere that is associated with an area or city, the Indian notion goes beyond and implies that it is a state of mind. Take the two instances of Montreal in Canada and Banaras (Kashi) in India. For example, Hugh MacLennan in his novel *The Watch That Ends the Night* has written so perceptively about Montreal that the city itself becomes the main character in the novel along with other human characters:

> It is a curious city, Montreal, and in this story I keep returning to the fact that it is. Strangers never understand its inner nature, and immigrant families, even from other parts of Canada, can live here two generations without coming to know it in their bones. I am absolutely certain that Montreal is the subtlest and most intricate city in North America. With her history she could not have been otherwise and survived, for here the French, the Scotch and the English, over two centuries have been divided on issues which ruin nations and civilizations, yet have contrived to live in outward harmony. This is no accident. They understand certain rules in their bones.[13]

In the Indian context, a city like Banaras (Kashi) becomes a symbol of spiritual life. Kashi is thought of not just as a city but it is a space in the heart of man—every man. That is why it is quite common to talk about *antara-kashi*, "the inner Banaras." In fact there is the Sanskrit saying "Kashi Kshetram Shariram tribuvana janani vyapini Jnana Ganga" (My body, the holy site, is Banaras—Spreading within me as knowledge, the Ganges,—

Mother of the three worlds). This concept of place emerges very clearly in the famous novel of Raja Rao, *The Serpent and the Rope*. In fact, even Eliot says: "the river is within us." Raja Rao says: "Banaras is everywhere where you are, says an old Vedantic text and all waters of the Ganges."[14] Again he points out "Ganges is ever so knowing, so wise. If wisdom become water the Ganges would be that water, flowing down to the seven seas." (43) In his writing Paris and Banaras become one as the rivers Ganga and Rhone attain a spiritual sangam: "Paris is a sort of Banaras turned outward and where but in Banaras would Baudelaire be more real, more understandable, more perfect, and in every dimension." (54) That is the reason why in Vedantic thought the world as a "place" is unreal like a city seen in a mirror. The world is within and it is only the projection of *Mayashakti*, the power of illusion that projects it outside. The great Shankara in his famous Hymn, *Dakshinamurti Stotram*, points out:

> Vishvamdarpanadrishyamananagaritulyam nijantargatam
> Pashyannatmani mayaya bahirivodbhutam yatha-nidraya.

These Sanskrit lines sound just as beautiful and meaningful in French:

> Telle une ville dans un miroir
> l'univers est contenu en Lui
> mais comme produit par mirage
> comme en songe
> et cependant existent an verite dans le Soi.[15]

An understanding of "Place" in these terms is what makes T.S. Eliot say:

> We shall not cease from exploration
> And the end of all our exploring
> Will be to arrive where we started
> And know the place for the first time.[16]

Again we find:

In succession
Houses rise and fall, crumble, are extended,
Are removed, destroyed, restored, or in their place
Is an open field, or a factory, or a by-pass. (123)

It is in this context of impermanence that Indian thought of the world as an "illusion" is to be understood. The world has only a physical, phenomenal, empirical reality without possessing the quality of Ultimate Reality. The former in Sanskrit is known as Vyavaharika Satta as different from *Paramarthika Satta.*

This introduction by way of giving a comparative theoretical background for the discussion of the concepts of Space, Time and Place should suffice. Now we shall turn to the two Canadian poems chosen for comment.

II

First, Bliss Carman's poem:

Lord of My Heart's Elation

Lord of my heart's elation,
Spirit of things unseen,
Be thou my aspiration
Consuming and serene!

Bear up, bear out, bear onward
This mortal soul alone,
To selfhood or oblivion,
Incredibly thine own,—

As the foamheads are loosened
And blown along the sea,
Or sink and merge forever
In that which bids them be.

I, too, must climb in wonder,
Uplift at thy command,—
Be one with my frail fellows
Beneath the wind's strong hand,

A fleet and shadowy column

Of dust or mountain rain,
To walk the earth a moment
And be dissolved again.

Be thou my exaltation
Or fortitude of mien,
Lord of the world's elation,
Thou breath of things unseen![17]

The "Lord" of heart's "elation" is a "Spirit" and it is a spirit of "things unseen," and the poet wants this "Spirit" to be his "aspiration." However, this elation bestowing "Spirit" is both "consuming" and "serene." For an Indian reader familiar with Hindu philosophical-Vedantic tradition, the first stanza "invocation" immediately strikes a familiar chord. The "spirit of things unseen" reminds one of the concept of "Nirguna Brahman." It is not only without attributes—"nirguna" but it is trans-sexual—not masculine, nor feminine nor is it neuter. This 'it' is 'that'—indicted by the word "Tat" in Sanskrit. Being a "spirit of things unseen," it is itself unseen and unseeable, because this "Spirit" is the transcendental Ultimate Reality which cannot be comprehended by the senses. That is why it is worthy of "aspiration," as it transcends both space and time. The transcendental Ultimate Reality is known as "Brahman" in Vedanta. This is what Emerson is talking about in his poem *Brahma*. In the present context the second stanza of the poem is relevant:

Far or forgot to me is near;
Shadow and sunlight are the same;
The vanished gods to me appear;
And one to me are shame and fame.[18]

The spacio-temporal level has to be transcended in order to comprehend the "subtle ways." The world of relativity which admits of "far and near," what is "forgot," what is happening and what is yet to come are only a result of "thinking." Their minds are circumscribed by the space-time limitation—*Desakalaparicccheda* which they have taken for granted—

Avicharitasamsiddha. The transcending of apparent opposites like far and near, then and now is what helps in understanding the true nature of Brahman who is beyond space, and time. As Archie J. Bahm sums up:

> In Hindu metaphysics, Shankara's *Nirguna Brahman*, the only ultimate reality, is timeless being. All events are illusory (maya), because they appear to have a being and nature different from *Nirguna Brahman*, but reality is nondual (*advaita*), so apparent events have no reality apart from timeless Brahman. Strictly speaking, we cannot attribute duration or even timelessness to Brahman either, since it is entirely without attributes (*nirguna*). But it always is, not in the sense of "always" as "at all times" but in the sense that it is whether anything else is or not. (58)

> Shankara, Advaita Vedantist, held that Brahman is the only Reality, that Brahman is nonspatial, that spatiality is a false appearance. "Space implies coexistence of a plurality of objects." But Brahman, or Reality, is one and indivisible. Therefore space is unreal. (71)

Naturally, the "elation" of the title of the poem "Lord of My Heart's Elation" is not mere mundane joy or worldly "happiness" but it is elevation—indeed an "exaltation" as is transformed in the last stanza of the poem. It is "serene" because it is pure and uncontaminated by human limitations—quite beyond the pale of words and meanings: "*Vagartha.*" It is indeed beyond even the reach of the mind: "*Yato Vacho nivartante aprapya manasa saha*" as the Sanskrit spiritual saying goes. Indeed, this is the "message"—the "vision" of the poem which is worked out in the next four stanzas which is brought to fruition in the final sixth stanza. However, the "aspiration" is not only "severe" but also "consuming." Unless the spiritual aspiration becomes a consuming all-absorbing obsessive passion, it is not worthy of being an "aspiration" or a goal, "*guri*" in Sanskrit. This goal or "*guri*" is what gives meaning to life without which life would descend into an atheistic, existential "hell." The "elation" that the poet speaks of therefore is "Ananda"—the supreme Bliss (which Bliss

Carman is experiencing if the pun may be pardoned!) which is paradoxically both "consuming and serene" at the same time. The second and the third stanzas have some quintessential words: "up," "out," "outward," "mortal," "soul," and "selfhood," "merge," "that," "be." The "Lord" of the "Heart's elation" is reached, attained through "sinking" the narrow personal ego "forever" and "merging" it into "oblivion" so that "selfhood" is achieved. It is not so much a conscious achievement as an awareness of consciousness which is the ever-present Self. In terms of the vocabulary of the poem, "this mortal soul" which is the individual identity must transcend the limited ego-sense or egoity and become "that." "That," which is known as "Tat" in Sanskrit is what everyone really is, in fact, which is, in fact one of the "Mahavakyas"—tat tvam asi (Thou art That). It is this "That" which bids them "be." Being is the Reality; becoming is a process which culminates in the ultimate knowledge of Being. The individual "foamheads" which are the individual souls "loosened and blown along the sea" must realize that the foam and the waves are but the sea and therefore "must sink and merge forever" in the universal, one and only Self with 'S' capital. The fourth and the fifth stanzas peruse and pursue the same idea through a different imagery. Notice the words "uplift," "climb," "one," "column," "dust," "mountain rain," ending up in "dissolve again." Whether it is through the element of water and the sea or through "shadowy column" or "the wind's strong hand" or "walking the earth,"—man must "uplift" himself "at thy command"—i.e., the "Lord of the Heart's" command and "merge for ever": "be one with my frail fellows" as there is only one spirit that is coursing through the various bodies which have different names and forms and through this universal humanism attain salvation. This, in terms of the poem, is to "climb in wonder." The sixth and final stanza neatly ties up all these thoughts by repeating and slightly altering the quintessential words used in the first stanza. The "Lord" of the individual "heart's elation" has become "the world's elation" and the "aspiration" has turned into "exaltation." The "Spirit of things unseen" has become the very "breath of things unseen" and this "Spirit," this "breath" is not only "my" elation and "my exaltation" but the 'I' has become "thou": "Be thou my exaltation"—an "*Advaita Siddhi*"—the achievement of non-dual experience. What is explored in this poem is basically the exploration of inner, interior space called "*Hridayakasa*" which results in the transcendence of the ordinary, physical, phenomenal, empirical, outer, outward "space." The inner, interior space is the "space" where Brahman resides and it is to this cave in the heart that the mind goes into during deep sleep and it surfaces again on awaking up. As Ramana Maharshi points out: "Brahman alone shines as 'I,' 'I,' in the Heart. It is the form of the Self."[19]

Margaret Atwood, in her poem "You Want to Go Back," explores through the concepts of Time and Space, the true nature of Man:

You Want to Go Back

You want to go back
to where the sky was inside us
animals ran through us, our hands
blessed and killed according to our
wisdom, death
made real blood come out.

But face it, we have been
improved, our heads float
several inches above our necks
moored to us by
rubber tubes and filled with
clever bubbles,

our bodies
are populated with billions
of soft pink numbers
multiplying and analyzing
themselves, perfecting
their own demands, no trouble to anyone.

I love you by
sections and when you work.

Do you want to be illiterate?
This is the way it is, get used to it.[20]

The first two lines are an opening gambit to explore the process of the evolution of man—biological as well as mental and spiritual. While "back" indicates time past, "inside" indicates "space." From the point of view of Indian philosophical thinking, Darwinian evolution is a false concept. The evolution is not so much from monkey to man, through the notorious "missing link" but evolution of man into a superman through the exercise of his intellectual process and through his essential spiritual nature. Margaret Atwood takes into consideration quite significantly, both the body and the mind in her poem. Paradoxical as it may seem, if we "go back" far enough, we will end up in the future. As Eliot has realized, "Time present and time past" are both present in "time future" and "time future" is contained in "time past." That is why he says:

What we call the beginning is often the end
And to make an end is to make a beginning.
The end is where we start from. (144)

The linear concept of Time has to yield place to the cyclical or circular and then the wisdom of "in my end is my beginning" and "in my beginning is my end" makes sense.

human kind
Cannot bear very much reality.
Time past and time future
What might have been and what has been
Point to one end, which is always present. (118)

I sometimes wonder if that is what Krishna meant:

Among other things—or one way of putting the same thing;
That the future is a faded song, a Royal Rose or a lavender spray
Of wistful regret for those who are not yet here to regret,

Pressed between yellow leaves of a book that has never been
opened.
And the way up is the way down, the way forward is the way
back.[21]

Atwood wants "you to go back." Not just to the immediate past but to such a time "where the sky was inside us." Notice the space-time continuum which is a prelude to spacio-temporal transcendence. Change the "where" into "when" and you have the answer. When exactly was the sky *inside us*? The answer—always. Where was the sky *inside us*? Always, because the sky, the air, fire, water and earth were always inside us and will always be. It is significant that the "Four Quartets" of Eliot have as their "source" the four elements of earth, water, fire and air. The elements are only empirically seen as being outside us but what is outside is exactly what is inside and thus man is but a conglomeration of elements and his body and his mind are what give a false notion about "inside" and "outside"—as well as "then" and "now." That is why in the ultimate analysis, space and time are only creations and projections of the concocting mind: "Maya kalpita desa kala kalana vaichitrya Chitrikritam" as the great Adi Sankara has said.

I am not at all implying that Atwood has heard of Shankara or has ever been familiar with Hindu philosophy. As has already been said at the beginning of this essay, this is how her poem makes sense and comes alive to an Indian reader. This is just one Indian response as there can be several. "The sky was inside us" is a familiar thought to an Indian—not only that "The sky is inside us" and "always" will be. "Sky," "Ether," "Space"—indeed, the entire inter-stellar space is "inside us" in microcosm and it is symbolic of the "macrocosm" which is usually assumed to be outside. The idea of "hridayakasa" (already referred to earlier)—the space within the heart—indeed in the cave or cavern of the heart—"hridayakuhara" is the in dwelling space of the infinite, eternal, all-pervading—That. The self in deep sleep sushupti when there is no consciousness of body or mind—is pure Consciousness—without the impediments of the knowledge of Space, Time and Place.

In another poem "The Woman Who Could Not Live with Her Faulty Heart," Margaret Atwood says:

> and at night it is the infra-red
> third eye that remains open
> while the other two are sleeping
> but refuses to say what it has seen.[22]

Indeed, the "third" eye which is always open is the sakshi, the "observer." In the words of another Canadian poet P.K. Page, we read:

> Who am I
> or who am I become that walking here
> I am observer.[23]

To "go back" to that state is the goal of life—and to remain there is the achievement. When Atwood talks about "animals ran through us" and "our hands," "killed according to our wisdom," she is contemplating on man's evolution through time as we see that she moves quickly from the animal existence to man's body-mind Consciousness.

> our bodies
> are populated with billions
> of soft pink numbers

Yes, but notice that Margaret Atwood in a typical ironic tone says:

> But face it, we have been
> improved, our heads float
> several inches above our necks.

As she has said in "Song of the Hen's Head,":

> The word is an O,
> outcry of the useless head,
> pure space, empty and drastic.[24]

Then comes "the overwhelming question"—Do you want to be illiterate? If all the manifestations of the "literate mind" and all its mischievous machinations are interested in "perfecting their own demands," then, what is the use of "our heads" floating "several inches above our necks"? The "head" should merge in the spiritual "heart-space" and that is why

> You want to go back
> to where the sky was inside us.

The Indian view of matter and mind differs from that of a philosopher like Descartes who is considered "father of modern philosophy." According to him through his "Je Pense, Donc Je suis"—*Cogito Ergo Sum*, since thinking is a part of mind's activity and Descartes discusses matter and mind in relation to space, Archie J. Bahm says: "A space, or intrinsic place, does not differ in actuality from the body that occupies it. . . . In reality the extension in length, breadth, and depth that constitutes the space is absolutely the same as that which constitutes the body." Matter and space are identical, and there is no empty space. But Descartes also held that matter is not all that exists, for spirit, mind, or consciousness also exists and it is not spatial." (70)

This experimental "explication de texte" of two poems—one traditional and the other modern—has been attempted only to indicate how many of the Canadian poets have passed through the stage of "survival" and "new Easts" have surfaced in their poems. It is perhaps not inappropriate to conclude by quoting a few lines from a Canadian "pilgrim" in India though she is not essentially, primarily a poet:

> Salutation to Him
> The great-souled One,
> Who has no name nor form.
> He who resides in all
> Who is Lord of all
> The Self of all beings.[25]

NOTES

1. *The Bhagavadgita*, Chapter IX, verse 32.
2. Sri Anandanubhava, *Padarthatattvanirnaya.*
3. Sri Shankaracharya, *Dakshinamurti Stotram*, verse 2.
4. Douglas Le Pan, "Coureurs de bois," qtd. *Canadian Literature in the 70s*, ed. Paul Denham and Mary Jane Edwards (Toronto: Holt, Rinehert and Winston, 1980), p. 13.
5. F.R. Scott, "The Canadian Authors Meet," *The Oxford Book of Canadian Verse in English and French*, ed. A.J.M. Smith (Toronto: Oxford University Press, 1960), p. 188.
6. "Book of Ancestors," *Canadian Literature in the 70s*, pp. 101-2.
7. Bliss Carman "Low Tide on Grand Pre," *The Oxford Book*, p.85.
8. A.J.M. Smith, Introduction, *The Oxford Book*, p. xxxiv.
9. *Canadian Literature in the 70s*, p. 117.
10. D.S. Subbaramaiya, *Sri Dakshinamurti Stotram*, Commentary (Sringeri, 1988), p. 325.
11. Archie J. Bahm. *Metaphysics—An Introduction* (1974; Harper and Row, 1986), p. 44.
12. T.S. Eliot, *After Strange Gods* (London: Faber and Faber, 1933), pp. 40-41.
13. Hugh MacLennan, *The Watch that Ends the Night* (Toronto: Macmillan, 1958), p. 255.
14. Raja Rao, *The Serpent and the Rope* (London: John Murray, 1960), p. 388.
15. Raja Rao, *Le Serpent Et La Corde* (Traduit de l'anglais par Georges Fradier. Calmann-Levy. Editeurs. 3, Rue Auber, Paris. c 1959).
16. T.S. Eliot, *The Complete Poems and Plays 1909-1950* (New York: Harcourt, Brace and World, 1952), p. 145.
17. *The Oxford Book*, pp. 90-91.
18. Emerson, *Brahma*, Stanza 2.
19. Ramana Maharshi, *Ramana Gita*, verse 17, trans. A.R. Natarajan (New Delhi: Affiliated East-West Press, 1995), p. 145.
20. *Canadian Literature in the 70s*, p. 99.
21. T.S. Eliot, *The Complete Poems and Plays*, pp. 133-34.
22. *Canadian Literature in the 70s*, p. 105.
23. P.K. Page, "Arras," *The Oxford Book of Canadian Verse*, p. 353.
24. *Canadian Literature in the 70s*, p. 102.
25. Elise Aylen, *The Night of the Lord* (Bombay: Bharatiya Vidya Bhavan, 1967), p. 55.

Major Trends in Modern Canadian Drama and Theatre

The word 'modern' is meant to indicate the latter half of the twentieth century as Canadian plays are being written since the eighteenth century. The object of this essay is not a chronological survey but identifying certain trends. A dozen playwrights and plays have been chosen for comment. The order in which they are commented on also are therefore not chronological.

The simplest definition of drama is lyricism plus mime, lyricism standing for words and mime for action—suiting the word to the action and the action to the word, to put it in Hamlet's words. For the present writer, the connection between drama and theatre is inalienable with the result that the words on the printed page are like the blueprint of a building on paper, to echo Tennessee Williams. The drama text therefore is a pre-text if not a pretext for performance. It is perhaps best to begin the discussion of modern Canadian drama with a quotation from a prominent modern Canadian playwright, Michel Tremblay, which sets forth the difference between the old and the new plays:

> I've ridden on the wings of the theatre for almost twenty years, from the Venice of the Doges to the bloody England of Elizabeth, from la noble France to Spain, proud and sombre! And all I saw was admirable! All that I heard was beautiful! And when the curtain fell after those fleeting hours of boundless happiness, my heart would stop, my life held captive behind the red velvet curtain. And I'd nourish myself for days on the substance of what had been granted me! But today, for the most part, especially in the so-called 'new culture,' the curtain doesn't even exist. Fini, the sacred mystery! Fini, the voyage of initiation! You walk into a theatre and the set hits you in the face! If the actors aren't there already waiting

> for you, mumbling their text or staring out at you, as if the characters in a play could see you! Yet, you having paid to look at, you've paid to look! And when the . . . play begins, they provoke you, insult you, cover you in filth. . . . Nothing is too vile, nothing too ugly, too low. The poor spectator is lured into the theatre and trapped there like a rat. They've even done away with intermission. And they shout in your face using language that would make your hair stand on end.[1]

This rather long passage has been quoted here to show how Michel Tremblay, a playwright of the 'new culture,' knows how to project the opposite point of view. He is a rebel playwright and an 'angry young man,' a counterpart of John Osborne of *Look Back in Anger* in England. He makes fun of the pretence of 'langue Francaise' used in the Outremont region of Montreal by purposely using joual which is very much the working class language of East Montreal. His social realism and protest in the play under consideration takes the form of an attack on the pseudo sophistication when he makes one of the four sisters marry 'below her social status':

> But Guido came into my life like a dagger thrust cleanly into the heart, making a beautiful sound that's clear, frank, precise! Freedom! An open window! Honesty! Ha! Guido's honesty, after all those years of courtesies, bows, kissing hands; of "Have-you-heard?" and "Oh, look at me!" I was carried off, like in a cloak and dagger movie, practically out of my bedroom window. My prince charming had an accent to make you shudder and nothing in his hand, but a rake, but God, he was beautiful and I loved him! I almost left Outremont on the seat of a tractor to become what sister Fernande calls common, as she holds her nose, but what I call real, laughing, singing and tapping my feet. (58)

Poetic drama is a comparatively rare genre and George Woodcock's *The Island of Demons* has been chosen as a representative. The ideal of poetic drama was set forth by T.S. Eliot in his 'Poetry in Drama' where he opines that the audience should not be too self-conscious of listening to poetry on the stage. Woodcock's play, since it has an allegorical level and is a 'modern morality' does not attempt to make it such that the audience can say 'I can speak like that too.' For example we find Roberval cursing Michel and Marguerite:

> You and your lover planned to run away
> Into the green shades of wilderness.
> There is your wilderness—that demon's island.
> You shall have all you need . . . your servant,
> Axes and spades, the tools to build a hut,
> Food of the flesh you shall not want.
> But in the spirit you may starve.
> No priest will ever join your hands,
> No holy baptist give your child a name,
> No blessed voices sing your orisons
> When you are laid within the alien earth.
> And if no visible demons send your peace,
> Do not forget the demon called Regret.
> There is the sentence.[2]

This Canadian play also evokes nostalgia for France in a sort of colonial consciousness:

> Lady, do you remember the country of your childhood,
> Those wide French plains swept golden with the wheat
> Breaking against the grey walls of cathedrals,
> The wandering streams, the woods, the evening gathering
> Over the mushroom meadows and the primrose lanes? (54)

The play *Balconville* is representative of an important aspect of Canada—its bilingualism. In fact, one third of the play is written in French. We move from English to French and vice versa all the time illustrating Hugh MacLennan's Idea of 'two solitudes.' The play ends with the following dialogue:

Paquette: Leve-toi . . . Leve-le
Johnny: Irene, he's speaking French!
Irene: Lift it!
Paquette: Tourne-le . . . Tourne-le . . .
Johnny: Yeah, yeah . . . tour-ney . . .
Paquette: A droite . . .

Irene: To the right.
Paquette: Laisse-le slyer sur la rampe . . . la rampe . . .
Johnny: What???
Irene: Slide it down the banister!
Johnny, Irene, Muriel and Tom: (turning to the audience) What are we going to do?
Paquette, Cecile, Diane and Thibault: (turning to the audience) Qu'est-ce qu'on va faire? Blackout.[3]

About *Zastrozzi: The Master of Discipline*, the author George F. Walker says:

> This play is not an adaptation of the novel *Zastrozzi* by Shelley. The author read a brief description of this novel in a biography of Shelley and that provided the inspiration for *Zastrozzi: The Master of Discipline*—something quite different from the Shelley novel.[4]

Zastrozzi is a German master criminal in whose world chaos is the natural condition and evil the most powerful motive force and crime is the meaningful action. He is to be contrasted with Verezzi, an Italian artist and a dreamer and the play tries to assert order and impose meaning in a world of chaos. The play is a combination of Shelley's Gothic Romance, Nietzsche's philosophy and Artaud's 'Theatre of Cruelty' written as a melodrama. The scene is placed in the 1890s. This play can be taken as an illustration for plays that are made out of earlier novels and plays. The same context continues when we look at the next play which is a spoof and a parody of Shakespeare.

Reworkings, parodies, sequels to Shakespeare's plays in the comic context are a legion. Specifically in the Canadian context the play *Goodnight Desdemona (Good Morning Juliet)*[5] by Ann-Marie MacDonald converts two of Shakespeare's great tragedies—*Othello* and *Romeo and Juliet*—into hilarious comedies. However, as the present writer has published an independent essay on this, it will not be commented on here. The present concern is a short play entitled *Shakespeare Revises a Play* by Pierre Berton. The play is a sort of "Deconstruction" of *Hamlet* with a difference! It may be called a subversive and satirical imaginary conversation about *Hamlet*:

> The scene takes place in the Globe Theatre, London. circa 1602. A production meeting is in session. Present are the Executive Producer, the Director, the Assistant Director, the Script Editor, two beautiful and leggy Script Assistants, an Agency Rep, a Public Relations man and a playwright, W. Shakespeare.[6]

The great fun of reading this play naturally depends on a good knowledge of *Hamlet* in the original. The so-called 'revisions' that are suggested in the light of which Shakespeare has to revise his play are all an integral part of the play that we know.

Some of the 'expert suggestions' given to the playwright may be mentioned here. The first suggestion is that a ghost should be introduced. The second suggestion: 'Have old Polonius tell his kid to be thrifty, never borrow money, that sort of stuff.' The third suggestion is that Claudius must be murdered by pouring poison in his ear! The fourth is that Ophelia ought to be a teenager. Even the psycho-analytical interpretation of Ernest Jones regarding the famous 'Oedipus Complex' is hilariously brought in. The fifth suggestion: 'We've simply got to hypo the ending . . . we got to give them a blood bath . . . Yeah! Daggers, swords, a cup of poison, maybe! The works! Corpses everywhere!' It is also suggested 'Have the Prince leap into a grave at one point and dig up an old skull or something.' This brief discussion is to show how the material which would have degenerated into a cheap blood and thunder piece is elevated to the level of a great play by the genius of Shakespeare.

A 'Docudrama' is both a documentary and a drama. The nature of the 'drama' is of course dependent on the nature of what it is documenting, and the mode of its presentation. The docudrama *Walsh*[7] by Sharon Pollock was premiered at Theatre Calgary on 7 November 1973 and was performed at the Stratford Festival in Stratford Ontario on 24 July 1974. The two-act drama with an interesting 'Prologue' contains within itself the historical background to understand this documentary—a recreation of history involving the States, Canada, and England. This triangle of trust and betrayal of the 'red' Indian by the whites is set forth in clear terms. As Jerry Wasserman points out:

> Walsh is grounded very firmly in historical fact. Major James Walsh did command the North West Mounted Police detachment that was charged with keeping order in the area that is now the southern Alberta-Saskatchewan border during the period (1877-81) that Sitting Bull and his Sioux spent there in exile. Two histories published the same year as *Walsh*, Grant MacEwan's *Sitting Bull* and C. Frank Turner's *Across the Medicine Line*, also confirm the basic accuracy of Pollock's presentation: the exemplary behaviour of the Sioux while in Canada, the great respect they developed for Walsh and the political machinations that eventually drove the survivors back across the line. (140)

Max Ferguson's *Remember the Good Old Days*,[8] though not exactly a play but just a skit, represents political satire in Canadian drama. The main character is Trudeau, the Prime Minister of Canada. Diefenbaker is also mentioned and so is Sir John A. MacDonald. The introduction says that "after several occasions on which the Prime Minister's earthy tongue had bruised the fragile psyches of Quebec truck drivers and various members of Parliament, Opposition Leader Robert Stanfield stated that his style was an affront to the office of Prime Minister." The scene opens with Trudeau "Tossing fitfully in his sleep while a raging storm hurls wind and rain against his window at the master bedroom at 24 Sussex Drive." A ghostly voice comes knocking at the door and announces: "Before the night is over . . . you will receive . . . three visitors. First . . . The ghost of Canada past . . . Then the ghost of Canada present. . . . and finally the ghost of Canada still to be. . . . Behold now. . . . The ghost of Canada past. Not well. . . . What he doth say . . . and learn how those who came before you. . . . Strove to ennoble and enshrine . . . the exalted office . . . which now you desecrate." The ghost of Sir John A. MacDonald comes weaving in saying "The Maple Leaf . . . our emblem dear. . . . Where is this libertine who would debase the highest office in the land?" (95-97) It is not so much what is said about Trudeau but how a piece of dialogue is written to go with an excellent cartoon.

Still Stands the House[9] by Gwen Pharis Ringwood is an excellent example of 'Prairie Drama' representing regional theatre. The attachment to land is the central theme. Though this can be construed as a universal phenomenon, the play particularizes it to such an extent that it is the Prairie itself which is the central character:

> The icy wind of a northern blizzard sweeps across the Prairie, lashes about the Old Warren farmhouse, and blows insistently at the door and windows. But the Warren house was built to withstand the menace of the Canadian winter and scornfully suffers the storm to shriek about the chimney corner, to knock at the door and rattle the windows in a wild attempt to force an entrance. (50)

The ubiquitous snow and frost present an oppressive atmosphere, including a bad blizzard in which both the husband and wife are tragically lost forever at the end of the play.

Preparing[10] by Beverley Simons is a remarkable one-act one-person play which spans the entire life of an archetypal woman in seven stages—seven ages. It is meant for a virtuoso performance by a great actress, with many exits and entrances, playing many parts from a schoolgirl to the final exit, as a shrouded corpse. The play has been discussed in detail in a separate essay. Sadhu Binning's *Lesson of a Different Kind*[11] may be mentioned in the context of writing by the immigrants. Binning is a founding member of Vancouver Sath and his plays are staged both in English and Punjabi. It pictures how the Sikhs who have settled in Vancouver and have good business establishment to exploit the working class Sikhs.

David French's *Jitters*[12] which was first performed in the Tarragon Theatre in Toronto on February 16, 1979 was directed by Bill Glassco. This play about a play takes into account all aspects of production like lighting, stage, speech including the cues and exit lines, the set, the costumes including the wigs, the play within the play, the script, the rehearsals, the stage props, the make up, the audience and theatre criticism. The discussion of this play brings us directly to the theatre context.

A brief review of the theatre scene in Canada may not be inappropriate here to bring together drama and theatre into a common fold. A summing up by Jerry Wasserman in the Introduction to his collection of Canadian plays can be presented here in conclusion.

> In 1952 Davies the playwright reacted with enthusiasm to the idea of a world-class Shakespeare festival theatre in Stratford, Ontario. Davies, along with Dora Mavor Moore, was instrumental in arranging for the innovative British producer-director Tyrone Guthrie to head the venture, which held its first season of two plays under a tent in the summer of 1953. Guthrie imported Alec Guinness and Irene Worth to play the leads and fleshed out the rest of the company with Canadian actors, a policy that by and large became standard for Stratford. . . . With support and encouragement from the Canada council a network of regional theatres spread across the country. Vancouver's Playhouse and Halifax's Neptune in 1963, Edmonton's Citadel in 1965 and Regina's Globe in 1966. By 1970 Montreal, Calgary, Fredericton and Toronto also had catering in principle to regional communities. . . . The building boom didn't stop with the regionals, either. To train and supply actors for the new national theatre network, the National Theatre School was opened in Montreal in 1960. At Niagara-on-the-Lake the Shaw Festival began operation in 1962. . . . In 1969, Kinch became a co-director of Toronto's Theatre Passe Muraille, founded the previous year by Jim Garrard. As its name suggests, Passe Muraille was to be a theatre without walls: neither the traditional fourth wall between actors and audience nor necessarily even the walls of a theatre building. Toronto was where most of the action was, and nothing did more to cement its position at the centre of the new movement than Tarragon Theatre, founded in 1971 by Bill Glassco. . . . Tarragon also introduces English Canada to the plays of Michel Tremblay with Glassco as director and co-translator. . . . There was a return to one of the original precepts of the regional idea, the commissioning of new plays by regional theatres by playwrights

with local roots and interests. These arrangements have proven mutually fruitful for playwrights and theatres alike. (17-18)

NOTES

1. Michel Tremblay, *The Impromptu of Outremont*, trans. John Van Burek (Vancouver: Talon Books, 1981), pp. 73-74.
2. George Woodcock, "The Island of Demons," *Two Plays* (Vancouver: Talon Books, 1977), p. 30.
3. David French, "Balconville," *Modern Canadian Plays*, ed. Jerry Wasserman (Vancouver: Talon Books, 1986), p. 309.
4. George F. Walker, "Zastrozzi: The Master of Discipline," *Modern Canadian Plays*, pp. 249-73.
5. Ann-Marie MacDonald, "Goodnight Desdemona: Good Morning Juliet" (Toronto: Coach House Press, 1990).
6. Pierre Berton, "Shakespeare Revises a Play," *Canadian Humour and Satire*, ed. Theresa Ford (Macmillan of Canada, 1976), p. 114.
7. Sharon Pollock, "Walsh," *Modern Canadian Plays*, pp. 139-68.
8. Max Ferguson, "Remember the Good Old Days," *Canadian Humour and Satire*, pp. 95-97.
9. Gwen Pharis Ringwood, "Still Stands the House," *The Prairie Experience*, ed. Terry Angus (Macmillan of Canada, 1975), pp. 50-74.
10. Beverley Simons, "Preparing," *Canadian Literature in the 70s*, ed. Paul Denham and Mary Jane Edwards (Toronto: Holt, Rinehart and Winston), pp. 83-97.
11. Sadhu Binning, "Lesson of a Different Kind," *Saclit Drama*, ed. Uma Parameswaran (Bangalore: IBH, 1996), pp. 84-98.
12. David French, "Jitters," *Modern Canadian Plays*, pp. 311-50.

National Image in Two Vancouver Plays by Sharon Pollock and Sadhu Binning

What Edmund Wilson says about Canadian nationalism, national building and creating the national image is very relevant in the context of providing the proper historical background and perspective for the discussion of the immigration policy and the Indian Diaspora in relation to the two Vancouver plays chosen for comment here. His book *O Canada: An American's Notes on Canadian Culture* was published way back in 1964:

> The Canadians have been debating in a rather academic way as to what it means to be a Canadian, without ever having been able to formulate a definition that is at all precise and that can be made to include everybody. And now the nationalist movement in French Canada is making this even more difficult. The British domination of Canada has never had a national flag—only the Red Ensign, as it is called, of the Canadian merchant marine, which has the Union Jack in the corner—while French Canada has employed as its emblem the flag of the Province of Quebec, a blue banner quartered by a thick white cross, with a fleur-de-lis in each corner. But now that British Canada's relation to England consists merely of belonging to the Commonwealth, an entity verbal rather than practical, and that the French Canadian nationalists are making it a point of honor to have a fleur-de-lis on their license plates, the new Liberal government of Lester Pearson is advocating a new, all-Canadian flag: three red maple leaves on a white background with—symbolizing the two oceans—a blue bar on either side. Mr. Pearson has not yet, as I write, been successful in getting Parliament to approve his new banner. . . .
>
> There seems to have been a similar problem in regard to the national anthem. The French sing a song called 'O Canada' and there is an English version of this, but the English have not always

> wanted to sing it. They have preferred 'God Save the Queen' or 'The Maple Leaf Forever,' which latter, on account of its reference to the defeat of Montcalm by Wolfe, is completely unacceptable to the French.

However, Wilson adds the footnote:

> Since this was written, Prime Minister Pearson has by closure put an end to the debate on the flag. The House of Commons, on December 15, 1964, by a vote of 163 to 78, approved the adoption of a new flag, though not the one described above. The committee to which the matter had been referred had proposed a different design: a single red maple leaf on white, with red bars instead of blue ones; and this is now to be the flag of Canada.[1]

In the context of nation building and national image in Canada it is appropriate to quote Robertson Davies, who, in his talk which he delivered in the United States on April 5, 1977, says:

> What do I mean when I speak of myth? In national terms I mean the sort of attitude which most people take for granted, the belief that nobody questions because nobody troubles to put it in concrete terms. The myth of national character is familiar to us all: in your country it is summed up in the figure of Uncle Sam, a Down-East Yankee in the dress of 1830 or thereabouts, totally unlike most of your citizens in every way, though now and then, on the streets or in a photograph, one spies the reality on which the stereotype was founded. We all know John Bull, who is not at all like any Englishman we have ever met, and Marianne, that generous-hearted, big-breasted female who is such an incongruous symbol for modern France. But where is the Canadian stereotype? We had one once, a grinning fellow called Jack Canuck, who looked as if he were engaged in wheat-farming on a large scale, but we got rid of him because he simply didn't do. Of late years two stereotype figures have arisen from the pressures of our political situation; one is a wistful, large-eyed, pitiful girl in the peasant dress of the eighteenth century, and the other is a coarse-grained, large-footed, evil-visaged Scotch banker, to whom she is bound in a hateful marriage from which she seeks to escape. The mismated pair are, of course, Quebec, La Belle Province, and the other part of Canada. A queer

> song-and-dance team they are. But whatever reality they may have in Canada—and certainly they have some roots in popular belief, which is not to say, roots in fact—they are not recognized outside Canada, and the essential point about national stereotypes is that they should have a wide acceptance among people of other nations.[2]

The national image as it emerges in two plays which are termed "Vancouver Plays" and are focussed here are: *The Komagata Maru Incident* by Sharon Pollock and *Lesson of a Different Kind* by Sadhu Binning. These plays deal with the Sikh immigrants and thus can be connected together.

While the former play is written by a Canadian playwright who has made a name for herself as an exponent of a part of Canadian experience which is normally not talked about, through her plays like *Walsh* and *Komagata Maru Incident*, establishing herself as a writer of powerful 'docudrama,' the latter is a play by an emigrant Sikh, Sadhu Binning who was born in Punjab, took his first degree in India and is a founding member of "Vancouver Sath," is on the editorial board of "Watan" and "Ankur," and teaches at the university of British Columbia.

II

The Komagata Maru Incident has been described as "a brilliantly imaginative and searing portrayal of a shameful and hidden chapter in Canadian history." The play was first produced at the Vancouver Playhouse in January 1976. Sharon Pollock, the playwright herself has written a "Note" in which she gives the historical background for her play:

> By the early 1900s the Canadian government believed it had devised an airtight method to virtually exclude immigration from Asia. In 1914, the Komagata Maru, a Japanese steamer, entered Vancouver Harbour carrying 376 potential immigrants of East Indian origin. The majority were veterans of the British Army, and all were British subjects. As such, they had right of entry to Canada guaranteed by their membership in the British Empire. However, they were forbidden entry by Canadian immigration officials.

> For the following two months, the Komagata Maru lay at anchor in Burrard Inlet, with those aboard suffering much deprivation, while political, legal, and racial skirmishes ensued. Inspector William Hopkinson of the Department of Immigration was instrumental in negotiations with those aboard and was involved in the formation of a ring of informers within the Sikh community.
>
> The Komagata Maru returned to India in the fall of 1914, leaving behind only twenty passengers who could prove former residence in Canada. The repercussions of the government's actions—the Budge Budge riot, the radicalization of those aboard, the vigilante action against informers, the death of Hopkinson, the execution of Mewa Singh—were overshadowed by the outbreak of World War One.[3]

Sharon Pollock's plays always reveal excellent craftsmanship and she adapts the very interesting mode of presentation in *The Komagata Maru Incident* by introducing a Master of Ceremonies who plays many roles and provides the historical background for this docudrama in the opening speech of the play:

> Hurry! Hurry! Hurry! Right this way, ladies and gentlemen! First chance to view the Komagata Maru! At this very moment steaming towards picturesque Vancouver Harbour. Yes sireee! The Komagata Maru! A first-class—let the buyer beware—Japanese steamer, 329.2 feet in length, 2,926 gross tonnage! Captained by one Yomamoto, remember that name. And Japanese crew, carrying a cargo of coal! And 346 Sikhs, count 'em! Plus 30 East Indians, religious affiliation unknown! Add 'em all together and what do you get? That is correct, sir! Give the man a cigar! Three hundred and seventy-six is the answer! Three hundred and seventy-six Asians, to be precise, and all of them bound for Oh Canada, We stand on guard for thee!
>
> This is Vancouver, ladies and gentlemen, the 21st day of May, nineteen hundred and fourteen. (1-2)

Sharon Pollock who writes in support of the plight of the Native American Indians in her play *Walsh*, in this play she writes in support of Indian Indians, especially the Sikh Community and she is absolutely unsparing in her criticism of White Canadian

Immigration policy. Again, she makes the stage manager figure, the Master of Ceremonies, say:

> I am telling you my fears—fears that affect each and every Canadian today. . . . I fear for my country, and I fear for my people. . . . I am not ashamed, nor should you be, to state that this is white man's country! And I can tell you that our British legacy, our traditions, those things that we hold dear, that we have fought and died for, is placed in jeopardy today by a massive influx of coloured foreigners!
>
> The class of East Indian that has invaded British Columbia is commonly known as Sikh—having been accustomed to the conditions of a tropical clime, he is totally unsuited to this country. . . . The less we speak of his religion, the better. Suffice it to say that unless his ridiculous forms of worship are relinquished, he is an affront to Christian community. His intelligence is roughly that of our Aborigines. He indeed belongs to a heathen and debased class. (26)

The discrimination against the Asian community is done in a very clever way as the people who were not admitted had a legal right to get into Canada as they were subjects of the British Empire. As the M.C says:

> In the land of his birth, the average Indian's wage is nine dollars a year. There—you see how we operate, Hopkinson? Never a mention of race, colour, or creed—and yet—we allow British subjects to enter; they are British subjects; we don't allow them to enter. (11)

This is done in every devious way by imposing a tax to be paid on entry—two hundred dollars per head to be paid before entry. However, a decision was made to allow twenty individuals to enter out of three hundred and seventy six as the people who were permitted to enter according to the immigration officials fulfilled the condition of the legality of their Canadian domicile. The play ends with the stranded people shouting "Jai Khalsa" a number of times and a character called Mewa Singh is so angry that he fires three times and kills Hopkinson for which we are told he will be hanged. The play ends with a very touching speech with Mewa Singh on the gallows:

> I am a gentle person, but gentle people must act when injustice engulfs them. Let God judge my actions for he sees the right and the wrong. I offer my neck to the rope as a child opens his arms to his mother. (71)

III

After the Komagata Maru Incident, the immigration situation in Canada changed. As Robert F. Harney points out:

> In 1947 Prime Minister Mackenzie King called a revival of the mass immigration to Canada that had been curtained during the depression of world war II. 'The objective of Canada's immigration policy,' he wrote, 'must be to enlarge the population of the country. It would be dangerous for a small population to attempt to hold so great a heritage as ours.'[4]

However, after forty years when Harney is reviewing the situation he says:

> Today the effects of forty years of mass immigration, tensions between Francophones and Anglophones, the unresolved issue of the rights of the indigenous people, the disruptive pseudo-ethnogenesis lurking in the regionalism of the West and the Maritimes, and the traditional fear of absorption by the United States interact to make survival of the Canadian polity a recurring theme in public discourse. (52)

But between the Fortyies and the Eighties, in spite of the fact that one of the purposes of Canadian Immigration Policy to protect the Pacific Rim from heavy Asian Immigration, a large number of Sikhs seem to have emigrated in the late 1960s and early 1970s as Tara Singh Bains points out in his *The Four Quarters of the Night: Life Journey of an Emigrant Sikh*:

> Visitors could come to Canada and apply for permanent residence after they arrived, and it wasn't long before almost every Sikh family had one or more relatives from India staying with them.[5]

Considerable amount of research has been carried out in the field of the South Asian Diaspora in Canada and even with particular reference to India by people like Norman Buchignani who gives a detailed bibliography of more than two hundred books and articles on the subject including a dozen of his own works. He comments:

> 1983 marks the eightieth year of South Asian settlement in Canada. Once a small, isolated community in British Columbia, they now number at least 310,000 people of South Asian origin are presently one of Canada's most rapidly growing ethno-cultural populations. . . . Most Adult South Asian Canadians are immigrants who have come to Canada since 1972. Immigration and settlement are consequently important phenomena in the South Asian Canadian experience. A number of studies have tried to describe the complex process of immigration, settlement and subsequent community-building.[6]

In the context of the present paper some of the publications directly related to it may be mentioned: "Indian Immigrants in Canada" (1968) by Michael Ames, his own "Conflict and Change in British Columbia Sikh Family Life" (1973), "Intergroup Conflict and Community Solidarity: Sikhs and South Asian Fijians in Vancouver" by Buchignani, "Canada and India" by Kartar Singh, etc. Specifically on the Komagata Maru Incident several articles have been published. For example G.S. Deol's "Voyage of the Komagata Maru and the Ghadar Movement," the Government of India "Report of the Komagata Maru" Commission Enquiry (1940), Hugh Johnson's "The Voyage of the Komagata Maru: The Sikh Challenge to Canada's Colour Bar" published by the Oxford University Press, Delhi (1975) are significant. There are several M.A and Doctoral dissertations dealing with the East Indian community in Vancouver. For example, A.M. Cassin's "Class and Ethnicity: The Social Organization of Working Class East Indian Immigrants in Vancouver" (1977), James G. Chadney's "The Vancouver Sikhs: An Ethnic Community in Canada" (1976), F.M. Bhatti's "East Indian Immigration into Canada" (1974) and Brij Lal's "East Indians and British Columbia's" (1976)[7].

IV

Uma Parameswaran, a leading Indo-Canadian writer and critic, identifies four faces in the personal histories of South Asian Canadians upto the 1980s:

> The Phases are: first, wonder and fear at the new world around oneself and nostalgia for the world left behind; second, an overriding impulse to survive in the new world that makes one immerse oneself in one's profession or family, and often precludes political or social participation in the larger society; third, after one has found job security, a turning towards organizational activity within one's own ethnocentric community; and finally, an active participation in the larger political and social arena outside one's own immediate community.[8]

It is in this context that the second "Vancouver Play," Sadhu Binning's "Lesson of a Different Kind" is briefly discussed here. It is indeed a lesson of a different kind from Komagata Maru Incident. In this one-act play in three scenes, Sadhu Binning, whose plays are staged both in English and Punjabi versions and who is a founding member of Vancouver Sath, pictures a very different kind of life of the working class Sikhs who are exploited by their own community who have settled in Vancouver and have good business establishments. Since the focus here is on the theme, the technique of the play is not taken into consideration. The play shows the Sikh boss exploiting helpless workers. As the Young Female Worker-2 says:

> Workers! You call these people here workers? Most of them are boss's family members, relatives or close friends who can't dare say anything against the boss's wishes and then there are people like you who are like empty shells just waiting to be thrown away on the garbage heap.[9]

Indeed, she points out that the boss is like any other white employer. Any troublemaker who tries to form the workers union is immediately dismissed and this is what happens to the Young Female Worker-2 who is told to "Just pack up your things and go right now" as she narrates to the reporter:

> The only logic an employer knows is how to make maximum profit. And the employers here know that the best way to exploit immigrant labour is to do it through their own people and as a result, you get this contracting system. (93)

She tells the reporter: "Regardless of what he gets from the owners, we get minimum pay. No benefits of any kind. No overtime. No holiday pay. No sickness pay. You can't even take a day off if the boss is not happy with you." (92) But that is not all. In addition to economic exploitation there is also sexual exploitation. As she herself confesses "Simply, if you are not a relative or friend's wife or sister, then you are fair game, you are expected to please the boss." (92)

Thus in the two Vancouver plays briefly surveyed here we get two different views of immigrants into Canada. The two plays have been chosen for a brief analysis to indicate the attitude to the national image of Canada as it emerges at two different stages in Canadian history.

NOTES

1. Edmund Wilson, *O Canada, An American's Notes on Canadian Culture* (New York: The Noonday Press, A Division of Farrar, Strauss and Giroux, 1964), pp. 44-45.
2. Robertson Davies, "The Canada of Myth and Reality," *Canadian Literature in the 70s*, ed. Paul Denham and Mary Jane Edwards (Toronto: Holt, Rinehart and Winston, 1980), pp. 1-17.
3. Sharon Pollock, "The Komagata Maru Incident," *Playwrights Canada* (Toronto, 1978), playwright's note.
4. Robert F. Harney, "'So Great a Heritage as Ours': Immigration and the Survival of the Canadian Polity," *Daedalus*, Sp. No. "In Search of Canada," Fall 1988.

5. Tara Singh Bains and Hugh Johnston, *The Four Quarters of the Night: The Life Journey of an Emigrant Sikh* (Montreal and Kingston: McGill-Queen's University Press, 1995), p. 124.
6. Norman Buchignani, "Research on South Asians in Canada: Retrospect and Prospect," *The South Asian Diaspora in Canada: Six Essays*, ed. Milton Israel (Toronto: The Multi-Cultural History Society of Ontario, 1987), p. 113.
7. *Ibid.*, "Bibliography," pp. 126-41.
8. Uma Parameswaran, ed., *Saclit Drama. Plays by South Asian Canadians* (Bangalore: IBH, 1996), Introduction, p. i.
9. Sadhu Binning, "Lesson of a Different Kind," *Saclit Drama*, p. 90.

South Asian Diaspora in Rana Bose's *Baba Jacques Dass and Turmoil at Cote-Des-Neiges Cemetery*

Rana Bose, born in Bengal, educated in the United States who moved to Montreal in 1977, is a Founding Member of Montreal Serai and has written and staged nine plays in English. Rana Bose, the Serai's main playwright, is an intellectual who has been influenced by the socialist ideologies of Badal Sircar and Utpal Dutt, and is widely read in literature and political science. In order to assess the South Asian Diaspora, it is necessary to remember that there were two phases of immigration. The first immigrants entered Canada in the earlier half of the twentieth century, majority of them being of the working class. The Eastern provinces saw an influx of immigrants from South Asia only in the second phase, i.e. 1960 onwards. The second phase consisted of highly educated professionals trained in India. Rana Bose belongs to this later phase.

In addition to the well known "Two Solitudes" in Canada there is now a "Third Solitude"—the Solitude of the South Asian Diaspora. The focus in this paper is on this third solitude with particular reference to Montreal. As Hugh McLennan points out in his novel *The Watch that Ends the Night*:

> It is a curious city, Montreal, and in this story I keep returning to the fact that it is. Strangers never understand its inner nature, and immigrant families, even from other parts of Canada, can live here two generations without coming to know it in *their* bones. I am absolutely certain that Montreal is the subtlest and most intricate city in North America. With her history she could not have otherwise survived, for here the French, the Scotch and the English, over two centuries have been divided on issues which ruin nations and civi-

> lizations, yet have contrived to live in outward harmony. This is no accident. They understand certain rules in their bones.[1]

Baba Jacques Dass and Turmoil at Cote-Des-Neiges Cemetery[2] is a remarkable play not only from the point of view of the discussion of diaspora but a very powerful indictment on a number of contemporary issues. There is irony, there is satire, and there is a great deal of anger. Rana Bose can be talked about as the present day 'Angry Young Man.' What John Osborne was to London in 1956, Rana Bose is to Montreal today. The play was successfully staged at the Centaur Theatre in Montreal in 1987. Right away in the first stage direction, the scene is set:

> 5.00 a.m. in the morning. Night sky outline over Montreal. . . . Sound of street traffic, distant siren—drunken yell (Ou est ce que mon miel, hosti) gets closer and louder—till Binoy gets fed up, goes to the window and shouts back: "Regardez, dans i'amoire, cholis!" (175-76)

This establishes the bilingual nature of Montreal. Indeed, one cannot talk about Montreal without the Francophone and Anglophone elements together. At this point a very interesting poem by A.M. Klein entitled "Montreal" which is partly amusing can be referred to exemplifying the bilingual context as the poem is a mixture of both French and English:

> Grand port of navigations, multiple
> The lexicons uncargo'd at your quays,
> Sonnant though strange to me; but chiefest, I,
> Auditor of your music, cherish the
> Joined double-melodied vocabulaire
> Where English vocable and roll Ecossic,
> Mollified by the parle of French
> Bilinguefact your air![3]

In the play under consideration there is a sprinkling of Hindi, representing the presence of the South Asian Diaspora along with French and Spanish. For example, Jacques says "Salud, Salud (Stops in his tracks). Hey, que pasa? Sab thik thak beta?"

(188) There are also a number of expressions in Hindi interpolated with English. For example "Bhai bara wrestlingwala chunga joke mar diya." (216) Hindi films are also referred to sarcastically 'Sachcha aur Jhutha'—that was the name of an Indian flick. It means Truth and Bullshit. The language question takes on a humorous turn when Mr. Fraser questions Binoy "Imitating Indian accent." (199) Binoy facetiously "assumes a very Indian accent" (199) purposely:

Mr. Fraser: What is your date of birth?
Binoy: 15th August 1947, Independence Day.
Mr. Fraser: Good, good. Do you speak Hindi?
Binoy: No, sir, but I do speak Hindi and I can of course speak Bengali, some Urdu, Assamese, Oriya. I also know a few words in Gujarati, Marathi and even some Punjabi . . . but as far as the Southern languages go I am not all that conversant. How many languages do you speak?
Mr. Fraser: (bowled over) Well, I'm English Canadian, eh, so I speak English of course Je parle francais, aussismais, our (excitedly) I can also speak American, yes (suddenly gets angry) but wait a minute. I am asking the questions. You are the one who has made the application to live in Canada. (199)

The question of immigrants is mentioned in the very first speech of the play. Binoy, the protagonist, says:

> Ramdas, Shiv Pandey's son, sat behind the glass booth, raking every new arrival with relentless questioning. Ramdas from whom girls would run away giggling, the clumsy son-of-a-bitch who drooled from his mouth every time he opened it was now sitting in the glass booth as Canadian Immigration officer! (176)

Binoy, through whom the events in the play unfold themselves is an immigrant who is a writer by profession. About the central character he is creating, Janet his girl friend remarks: "You Indians are so corruptible. Tell me, why does your hero have to be so guilt ridden?" (177) to which Binoy replies: "The big deal Jan is that there is a lot of guilt—guilt is in the minds of the Indian soul, all right—guilt is in the Vedas—guilt is in the Puranas, and by the way it is also Biblical—guilt is rampant." (178) Rana Bose has created an extraordinarily interesting character in Binoy's mother who doesn't understand her son's attitude. However, she has been made thoroughly comic as she is continuously speaking only in well-known proverbs. That is her English. For example, "You're lucky you have a mother . . . a bird in hand is worth." (180) "Giving you advice is like casting pearls at the swine." (180) "You are now scribbling fiction on pieces of yellow paper. Nero fiddles while Rome burns." (181) "What is sport to the cat is death to the rat." (181) "It takes two to tango!" (182) "People in glass houses should not throw bricks at each other." (183) "Those who spit against the wind, spit in their own faces." (184) "As the wind blows so must you set sail." (185) Commenting on her characteristic style, Baba Jacques says:

> She is crazy. I don't ever wanna see her (unsettled) I never wanna see her—one time she told me I run with the hare and hunt with the hounds. What's that mean (Binoy laughs), you're not crazy like her. Do you also speak in proverbs? (190)

Even Janet makes fun of the language of Binoy's mother: "As she says blood runs thicker." (208) Some more examples of Ma's pronouncements are: "Well, as they say better late than never." (220) "We should never count the chickens before the eggs are hatched." (220) "One swallow does not make a summer." (220) "I don't let the grass grow under my feet." (220) "Do maggots like rotting flesh?" (231) "You cannot fit a square peg into a round hole." (239) This is one of the devices employed by Rana Bose to create comedy in the play *Baba Jacques*.

The entire Scene V can be taken up for a separate discussion where we see Rana Bose at his best when he is describing the cocktail party at an Indian home with all his wit, sarcasm, irony, humour and satire where everything from politics to immigration, petty party talk to the status of Indians abroad is mercilessly assailed. Just one example:

Soni: Aw come on Puri, you've had one too many.

Puri: Oh no! Let me tell you something Soni (licking his lips).
Soni: Oh yeah. Tell me something!
Puri: There's something about this country that is very different.
Soni: What is it?
Puri: I almost don't feel like . . . you know what I mean . . . I don't feel like a . . . like an immigrant any longer.
Soni: What do you feel like?
Puri: Like a Canadian . . . a natural born Canadian—you know it is very sacred feeling . . .
Soni: Like a sacred cow?
Puri: A what?
Soni: A sacred cow.
Puri: The sacred cow, yes . . . important, accomplished and reliable.
Soni: An immigrant cow!
Puri: No a citizen cow in a multicultural Canada.
Soni: Well-fed and respected.
Puri: And tolerated.
Soni: And appreciated. (223)

The party talk also involves the mentioning of an interracial marriage between a Canadian and an Indian. Indian culture subsists on covering up reality—ugliness is cloaked with godliness and spirituality—it is a world of lies." (228) Since it is a cocktail party there is plenty of party talk:

Puri: Arey, drink it—it is like Mataji's lassi back home!
Woman 1: Mataji's lassi did not have any rum, silly!

At this point Mrs. Tory lets out a very affected laugh and spills some drink on her blouse. Mr. Tory gets some Kleenex and starts wiping her chest. She says "James!" Puri tells Soni: "Alcohol does not leave any stains sir, Bhai, joke maar diya." (211)

Mrs. MP: (a little tipsy—sitting next to Tory MP and laughing loud) You know Mala, what really attracted me to Warren was the fact that he never really wanted to sleep with me before we got married. Now that's what! . . .
Tory MP: (feeling like a wimp) Well! I was kind of wary, you know, because of the rather conservative traditions of Indian culture. (212)

Woman 1: (puts her sari to her nose) Arey chi! chi! Mut bob aur . . . (both start laughing) but what do you think about those two . . . (looks towards Neela).
Woman 2: He is making the moves on her (her eyes flutter).
Woman 1: But he better watch it, cause she will hit him for a home run (both laugh). (227)

As Uma Parameswaran points out: "Montreal and Vancouver are the two major centres of south Asian Canadian theatre but they are quite dissimilar because of their immigration history. . . . The eastern provinces saw an influx of immigrants from South Asia only in the second phase of immigration, 1960s onward. The second phase consisted of highly educated professionals trained in India or in other erstwhile British colonies. . . . Rana Bose's *Baba Jacques Dass and Turmoil at Cote-des-Neiges Cemetery* is so packed with subtexts that much of it might get lost when staged . . . The Montreal Serai is motivated by forces within the community. They are motivated by patterns of racism endemic to the Canadian system and they react to forces generated by structures outside their heritage culture. Their plays consist of a multicultural cast and deal with problems common to minorities, though examples used are often from the South Asian Canadian experience." (vi-xii)

Binoy the protagonist writer confesses: "I unfold the story of the simple emigration of a middle class family to Canada" (181) to the objection of his mother: "Your father would have turned around six times in his grave if he found out that his only son had taken to a literary career leaving behind a brilliant engineering career." (181) This is significant in the context of how the second wave of emigration consisted of highly educated, technically qualified Indians. The point is further stressed when Binoy's mother points out: "Your father was an M.D. Ph.D. Your sister is a Ph.D., your brother-in-law is no less than a Professor in Biochemistry. Your Nitu uncle is a P. Eng. . . . Your Uncle Belu is also a Ph.D. and has his own company with branch offices in London and Kuwait" (181) to which Binoy replies sarcastically: "My cousin Shubhra is no less. She is teaching genetics at Toronto." (181) This point has been made here to show that the emigrant Indians are very highly qualified intelligentsia and their emigration to Canada as well as to other Western countries indicates an aspect known as "Brain drain." However, Baba Jacques of the title of the play is the other side of the picture. He is a French Canadian who is fascinated by India and who is spiritually oriented. Though Binoy is cynical about this and asks: "Couldn't he for once step out of his little Nirvana in Cote-des-Neige?" (184) Neela, Binoy's sister, replies:

> It is not Nirvana (shouting) Binoy, you know, sometimes your arrogance and ignorance appalls me! Jacques has nobody he can talk to about his one great passion—which is India—and you! You are neither here in Canada nor there in India, but pretending to be everywhere. There is something about India that is so timeless and without Jacques I would never have known. (184)

There were a number of comments made by Binoy which are severely critical of India. For example:

> Indians have built a poisonous cobweb of ideas around themselves. It is a defence mechanism. If you ask them why everybody is so poor in India, they will say "but culturally we are rich." A virtue is made out of poverty—which the "outsider" can never comprehend. (227)

To give a glimpse of Indians in Canada, just one more defensive remark by Binoy should be quoted:

> You are no less an Indian if you question the immensity of the destitution. If you tell Pun that more than 65% of India's population live below the poverty line—he will say that India has the third largest pool of engineers and technicians in the world. If you tell him why should 300,000 Indian children die every year from measles when a single dose of vaccine costs less than 20 cents, he will say Indian ayurvedists extracted the first blood pressure medicine 2,000 years ago. (228)

Scene II shifts to the Cote-des-Neiges Cemetery. "Night Outline of Montreal Mountain with cross. Bell music. Very dark dim lighting. Like a blue haze. Mysterious. In the background . . . vaults lying side by side with numbers on them. Some tombstones in the background." (185) The play "Baba Jacques" in spite of its stark realism has a surrealistic atmosphere. There are a number of sacrilegious jokes against things Indian by Binoy who is described as an 'agnostic.'

> You know, last night I dreamt I was in the mountains near Rishikesh. I did not see a single sadhu. . . . Actually I was there to have my Kundalini rise up in me and shatter through my forehead. (185)
>
> And you may ask me why the hell am I here—do I also suffer from some turmoil? Is it because you've convinced me to resolve the inner shit before I deal with the shit in the outside world? (laughs) And out here suddenly in this fake eeriness in Cote-des-Neiges cemetery, in Montreal, . . . I've met my destiny. . . . I'm about to give up my rotten materialistic past and join Jacques . . . (laughs) . . . and you my sister you are discovering a spiritual India, an India you were not even born in . . . and through the eyes of who but Jacques again (laughs) Jacques the Quebecois, hippy, fatherless in the eighties, he is our only source of the information on the old country because our parents won't tell us nothing. (186)

There are certain references to political events in India and Canada which are brought together as parallels. For example:

Jacques: Well . . . you know the October crisis. . . . Trudeau's state of siege.

Binoy: Of course I do, I was already here.

Jacques: Well there was a crisis in India in 75.

Binoy: (Jumps up). Yes of course the Emergency—tell me about . . . were you there?

Jacques: Yes. It made the October crisis look like an incident in an alley. (191)

Since Binoy is a writer and an angry young man at that he makes certain remarks about the publication business. He remarks:

> No matter what you say about the British, they're not [fucking] shallow. . . . In fact, I was just telling Neela the other day . . . that I would like it if the book got published in England . . . and she said a group of publishers there are looking for new works by Indian writers that could be sold and the money would be sent to Bhopal. (235)

There is also an incidental criticism of American publishing. He remarks that to be accepted by an American publisher if he "could add something like the Maharani of Jaipur was financing the contras with hash . . . from Iran, while her granddaughter was having a steady romance in Honduras with a contra leader . . . something like that would sell." (234) There are many parodies which are hilarious. In fact, the very first appearance of Baba Jacques is hilarious: "Jacques appears from a tunnel of light. Long hair, big beard with a bad toothy smile. Muttering a sloka. (Om Mani Padme Om)" (188)

The play *Baba Jacques* has everything to make it a success on the stage. It has even very interesting visual effects that have been worked into the stage directions including an element of the appearance of the ghosts because after all a part of the play takes place in a cemetery where Baba Jacques lives with the ghosts. Scene II of the play is placed in the cemetery. The stage direction reads:

> The night outline of Montreal, Mountain with cross. Scene in Cote-des-Neiges cemetery. Shaft of light at a raised level. Bell music. Very dark dim lighting. Like a blue haze. Mysterious. In the background . . . vaults lying side by side with numbers on them. Some tombstones in the background. (185)

There is a certain atmosphere which is surrealistic though it is handled in eerie comic context. "Neela goes over to vault 49 and opens it. An ashen faced woman in a long white gown steps out. Lights dim elsewhere." (182) The following stage direction makes the point quite clear:

> Noise of knocking comes from one of the vaults. Whispered voice: "Hey! You open the latch here . . . hey you, here number 38, here.

> hurry up." . . . Neela walks closer, puts her ears to 38, hears the whisper again: "Here, open it, open it." As soon as Neela opens a wiry looking white man with a moustache and black frame glasses leaps out yelling: "Free, free, free at last, Lord . . . free at last . . . On his knees." (197)

There are ghosts galore! There is an incredible combination of levity and seriousness in the play as it discusses the immigration policy of Canada on the one hand and the misunderstanding if not total lack of knowledge about India on the part of the Canadians. For example:

Esther: Do you have sex (she giggles) like in the Kam Soot?
Binoy: Not Kam Soot, ma'am, *Kama Sutra*. (193)

Rana Bose shares some of the anger of the Montreal rebel playwright Michel Tremblay when he says "Jan, my story is not about the gentle folks who live in Dollard-des Ormeauz or Laval on the Lake." (178) In the same way, Tremblay talks about Outremont section of Montreal. Indeed, Bose actually mentions Tremblay at one point in the play when he makes Binoy say:

> What is self-indulgence? Can you imagine and he's not even your regular Canadian writer with a name like Tremblay or McPherson. And how obscure can the subject be? I mean who cares about growing up in Montreal with Indian parents, who don't want to have nothing to do with their past or the present for that matter, except some vague shit about retaining one's heritage and culture. (208)

There is a reference to writers like Paul Scott and Bharati Mukherjee as the protagonist of the play happens to be a writer. About Baba Jacques, a number of details about his association with India emerge in the course of the play. For example:

Hostess: I thought he was a hippy.
MA: Yes, all the hippies who remained hippy are dangerous.
Hostess: What do you mean?

MA: He went to India in 1972—you know, these (walking a little) misguided youth of the west—smoking merrijana in Kathmandu and lying naked on the beach in Goa.

Hostess: Not Merrijana—marihuana . . . bahen.

MA: Yes, they also call it grass . . . but anyway—grass, weed, whatever he had—I heard India had a profound effect on him . . . he felt Western youth were ignoring India's poor and romanticizing philosophy and culture and past. (229)

Whatever the opinion of Binoy in the play or of the author Rana Bose, the present writer would like to say that he has himself personally met many of the hippies in Goa in the 60s and 70s and found some of them extraordinarily intelligent, well-read and well-informed people who were simply rebelling against the restrictions against their personal freedom in the West. Thus, he has sympathy for Baba Jacques, however freaky and strange he may seem to be. Like John Osborne's Jimmy Porter, Binoy of Rana Bose attacks everything under the sun, including Montreal, the city of his choice, when he makes a parody of the television reporter:

> Nick recounts saying good morning to him, while a deranged looking man with curly hair was seen prowling around at the back towards Dorchester. Station 25 policeman James D'arcy later said that they had put together a composite and were on the lookout for a man from the St. Henri district who was known to be prowling the Crescent Bishop neighbourhood in the early hours of the morning. . . . (Turns to the audience) It's here, folks. In the heart of our city in Downtown Montreal. Like an epidemic, like you've never seen it before, an alien spirit has descended on our fair city . . . and I tell ya—this city is turning the way of Toronto . . . growing levels of unscrupulous immigration have led to acute job shortages. . . . Youth from St. Henri and Cote-des-Neiges districts are prowling in the downtown subways. . . . Restless, jobless and with only their blasters to comfort them. . . . Montreal is shaping up for a hot summer. (201)

In this play, there is incidental negative references to the city of Toronto. At one point in the play we are told that Binoy is beaten up in Toronto. Scene IV of the play is placed in the Subway at

Toronto and "Binoy gets violently beaten up. Subway train roars by with lighting effect." (210) We get to know more about Toronto in Bose's play *Five or Six Characters in Search of Toronto*. However, any further comment on Toronto is outside the scope of the present essay. Uma Parameswaran points out: "Each of Bose's plays is a delight to read. In *Baba Jacques*, there is a sheer exuberance of imagination; the French Canadian mystic lives in the cemetery, and a stage full of characters—journalist Matt, Esther Crawford whose family owns a brewery and publishing house, bigoted Mr. Fraser—walk in and out of their vaults; the structure and stylistic techniques of the play are influenced by classical tradition and contemporary experimentation; the central thrust of the play is definitely a satirical look at South Asians' view of life in Canada and other Canadians' view of South Asians in Canada." (xvii)

In approaching South Asian Canadian theatre, one needs to understand two historical Indian bases to the theatre of protest developed by South Asian Canadians. One, this genre owes its format to the people's theatre movement in Bengal led by Badal Sircar, and the Marxist movement in India in the earlier decades of this century. Two, it uses many of the standard stage techniques and strategies used by folk theatre in India over the centuries. Thus, we must remember that while the plots move around the problems faced by South Asians and other "visible minorities" in Canada, many of the stage techniques are a transplant from India's folk and popular traditions. (v)

NOTES

1. Hugh MacLennan, *The Watch that Ends the Night* (Toronto: Macmillan of Canada, 1958), p. 255.
2. Rana Bose, "Baba Jacques Dass and Turmoil at Cote-Des-Neiges Cemetery," *Saclit Drama Plays by South Asian Canadians*, ed. Uma Parameswaran (IBH, 1996), pp. 174-242.
3. A.M. Klein, ed., "Montreal," *The Oxford Book of Canadian Verse in English and French* (Toronto: Oxford University Press, 1965), pp. 260-61.

Postcolonial Scenario in the Plays of Sharon Pollock and Gurucharan Das

While the exact nature of the colonial consciousness may change its scenario from country to country, the consciousness itself is a common historical heritage of the erstwhile colonies. Whether it is the British or the French, the Spanish or the Portuguese, the colonial memories and influences, attitudes and prejudices persist and change. Canada being a bilingual nation, came under the influence of France as well as England while India being a sub-continent came under the influence of Britain, and to some extent France and Portugal too. Pondicherry and Goa, have their own relationship with and influence of France and Portugal. For the purposes of the present paper, only two representative "historical" plays are taken into consideration for a brief comment to illustrate the changing global perspective with particular reference to Canada and India—Sharon Pollock's *Walsh* and Gurucharan Das's *Larins Sahib*.

To focus the changing colonial perspective, it may be a good idea to begin the discussion with a reference to George Woodcock's *The Island of Demons*. Woodcock, internationally recognized as one of Canada's most important and influential writers is a Member of the Royal Society of Canada and his plays, *The Island of Demons*, a Canadian Legend, and *Six Dry Cakes for the Hunted*, a Canadian Myth, have given him a significant place among dramatists. *The Island of Demons*[1] is relevant for the present discussion because the story of Michel and Marguerite is told in the context of French colonial history. The action of the play takes place on board a ship and on a remote island but the background is the "empire" of France and her colonies. However, Woodcock has elevated the play by universalizing human experience while tapping the rich resources of the French colonial consciousness. Marguerite's sense of regret is worked out in terms of evoking nostalgia for her French past:

> Lady, do you remember the country of your childhood
> Those wide French plains swept golden with the wheat
> Breaking against the grey walls of Cathedrals,
> The wandering streams, the woods, the evening gathering
> Over the mushroom meadows and the primrose lanes. (54)

Colonial consciousness is made to work at a deep-seated subconscious level here. As the play is a "Poetic Drama" and is basically symbolic and allegorical in mode, further comment is unnecessary. It is enough to establish it as a significant Canadian play to provide the general background illustrating colonial consciousness.

In a sharp contrast to this allegorical mode, Sharon Pollock's *Walsh* is a stark documentary of historical incidents, depicting the relationship of Canada with the native Indian Sioux. As Jerry Wasserman points out: "*Walsh* is grounded very firmly in historical fact. Major James Walsh did command the North West Mounted Police detachment that was charged with keeping order in the area that is now the southern Alberta-Saskatchewan border during the period (1877-81) that Sitting Bull and his Sioux spent there in exile. Two histories published the same year as *Walsh*, Grant MacEwan's *Sitting Bull* and C. Frank Turner's *Across the Medicine Line*, also confirm the basic accuracy of Pollock's presentation: The exemplary behaviour of the Sioux while in Canada, the great respect they developed for Walsh and the political machinations that eventually drove the survivors back across the line."[2]

This "Docudrama" which was premiered at Theatre Calgary on November 7, 1973 was also performed at the Stratford Festival in Stratford Ontario on July 24, 1974. It recreates colonial history involving the United States, Canada and England. The triangle of trust and betrayal of the 'red' Indian by the whites is set forth in very clear terms. As Gall says in the play:

> My grandfather was a soldier for the grandfather of Queen Victoria. At that time, your people told him that the Sioux nation belonged to that grandfather of the Queen. My people fought against the Longknives for your people then. We were told that you would always look after your red children. Now the longknives have stolen our land. We have no place to go. We come home to you asking for that. We come to you asking for that protection you promised.[3]

For the Indian, a promise is a promise—it is sacred. The changing political-colonial scenario and relationship between England and America does not concern him. He does not understand why this should affect the word that has been given to him. The great white Mother's Law has yielded place to the Law of "The President in Washington." Changing colonial perspectives are totally alien to him. Sharon Pollock lifts this docudrama to the stature of tragedy—a personal tragedy of Walsh who has to choose between his duty as a professional soldier and his own feeling of honesty, integrity, friendship and trust. His anguish is very effectively brought out when he says:

> I've always been a man of principles, Harry. I've always thought of myself as a man of principles . . . Honor, truth, the lot . . . They're just words, Harry. They don't exist. I gave my life to them and they don't exist. (102)

The only such other play in the colonial context which discusses trust and betrayal in the historical-tragic perspective is Peter Shaffer's *The Royal Hunt of the Sun*.[4] The colonial context there is of Spain in relation to Peru, thus providing another colonial context for the present discussion. The dilemma and conflict in the mind of Pizarro between the colonial professional interests, Spain in this instance and personal loyalty and a gentleman's word of honour to the Peruvian Indian Inca—this conflict is not dissimilar to Walsh's duty to his country and loyalty to his Sioux Indian friend.

Eugene Benson, talking about *Walsh* as a "historiographic metadrama" places it in the context of the Riel Trilogy—*Fortune* and *Men's Eyes*, *The Ecstasy of Rita Joe* and says the three plays represent "a radical revision of imperial history as any in Canadian drama" and suggests: "A British play examining British/ Indian relations with Subhas Chandra Bose as its hero/ protagonist would provide a reasonably close parallel."[5] However, there is a "reasonably close parallel" in a play which examines British/ Indian relations—Gurucharan Das's *Larins Sahib*: "It is 1846, seven years after the death of the formidable Maharaja Ranjit Singh, and the Sikh Kingdom has suffered a crushing defeat at the hands of the East India Company. Henry Lawrence, already a legend on the North-West Frontier, is appointed the Company's Agent to the Government of the late Maharaja's boy son, Dalip Singh. Preferring Indian officers to British in an attempt to restore Sikh self-respect, and endeavouring to root out corruption in the court, Lawrence alienates his superiors."[6]

This provides a definite and unmistakable changing perspective on colonial consciousness in the context of the imperialistic global perspective. Lawrence, the "Larins Sahib" is seen to be different from what he is expected to be by the "Pukka" Sahibs. His appearance in the Governor General's Durbar shatters the "Brandy—and elevenses atmosphere and the occupants of the room look suspiciously as if they are about to receive a stranger from another land and not one of their own race." (3) However, the brother of Lawrence, John, who is also in India in service is contrasted with Lawrence. John is the "regular sort—efficient, proven record" and above all, he "doesn't mix with the natives." From the point of view of the changing colonial perspectives in the colonial history, this contrast between the two brothers is most significant. Henry Lawrence, the "Sahib" of the play, though he is "the Lawrence of Punjab" (2) is the wrong Lawrence because he is "practically a native" (2):

> He doesn't look a soldier although he is one. He wears his regimental uniform, but not smartly; his boots could be better polished, his hair could be better combed. His face is burned almost as black as a native's and but for his uniform, he might easily be mistaken for a North Indian. (3)

In fact, Currie in the play calls him a "clown' and an 'Oriental.' They seem to be synonymous in the mind of this British imperialist. The dialogue between the two of them is revealing:

Currie: A word of advice, Mr. Lawrence. I hope you will restrain your orientalism and keep the natives at a distance. Keep them in their place if you have to rule them.

Lawrence: Who' going to rule anyone? His Highness Dalip Singh is the Maharaja. His mother is Regent. Sardar Lal Singh is the Wazir, I am merely the agent of a friendly power. (11)

Thus the idea of the changing colonial consciousness on the part of an imperial colonizer is depicted in an Indian play. However, the fact of colonial history of the 19th century is brought out in the Afterword of the play in the postcolonial historical context:

> Henry Lawrence was transferred to Rajasthan from the Punjab, a demotion in the eyes of his contemporaries. His younger brother, John Lawrence succeeded him in the Punjab and rose brilliantly to become the famous Lord Lawrence, the Governor-General and Viceroy of India. Henry Lawrence flickered once more briefly into history when he died defending the Residency in Lucknow in 1857 Mutiny. Much was made at the time of his heroism; some even said that he had saved the British Empire. (87)

Whatever the course of the Colonial history in India, Canada or elsewhere in the Commonwealth, the changing colonial scenario is a significant aspect of literary experience also. The discussion can be rounded off with reference to the local colour of Goa in Asif Currimbhoy's play *Goa*, another "historical play" like *Walsh* and *Larins Sahib*. Speaking about Currimbhoy, Faubion Bowers says: "Currimbhoy is India's first authentic voice in the theatre. He has written that country's first plays of dissent. He presents life as it is, not as something it should be."[7] Whether one agrees with this judgement or not, in the present context of the discussion of postcolonial consciousness in Canada and India, the relationship of Portugal with India is best represented in this play. It is true that the play *Goa* is not only about this aspect—perhaps not even mainly about it as it can be argued with reference to the symbolic element as indicated in the speech of to the symbolic element as indicated in the speech of Senhora Miranda when she says about her daughter. "She is Rose. And Rose is Goa; and Goa is Rose." (63) However the characters of Portuguese Administrator and Goan Nationalist are significant in the context of change in colonial perspective. As Portuguese Administrator says: "This is Goa . . . my home, no less than Lisbon where I was born. And we, the Portuguese came to India almost four centuries ago, we made Goa an enclave. . . . Ah, but my friend here, who calls himself a . . . a . . . Nationalist insists we made this into a . . . colony . . . instead of a small part of Portugal." (11) The Goan Nationalist says: "There is a change coming . . . inevitably. And my friend, you will be in the midst of it." (37)

As was stated at the beginning, whatever may be the special context of the colonial consciousness—that of Canada to France or England, that of India to Britain or Portugal, the attitude to the spirit of European colonization and the change that is taking place in the various Commonwealth countries—the erstwhile colonies—presents an extremely interesting and complex picture in recent Commonwealth literature.

NOTES

1. George Woodcock, "The Island of Demons," *Two Plays* (Vancouver: Talon, 1977).
2. Jerry Wasserman, ed., *Modern Canadian Plays* (Vancouver: Talon, 1986), p. 140.
3. Sharon Pollock, *Walsh* (Vancouver: Talon Books, 1986), p. 44.
4. .Peter Shaffer, *The Royal Hunt of the Sun* (London: Pan, 1969).
5. Eugene Benson, "Writing Canadian Drama in Colonial Space. Interrogation and Subversion," *Indian Journal of Canadian Studies*, Number 1, 1992, p. 85.
6. Gurucharan Das. *Larins Sahib* (Oxford University Press, 1970), Publisher's Note.
7. "Goa," *Asif Currimbhoy's Plays* (New Delhi: Oxford and IBH, 1972), Introduction, p. xii.

Beyond Feminism: Ann-Marie Macdonald's *Goodnight Desdemona* (Good Morning Juliet)

"Others abide our question—thou art free" was said of Shakespeare. He is free for all! It is difficult to say what has not been done to him. The plays that are born out of his plays are numerous. Shakespeare, among other things has been a jumping off place for other plays. Variations, adaptations, spoofs, parodies, interpretations, re-workings, sequels are a-plenty. To name just a few recent ones—Tom Stoppard's *Rosencrantz and Guildenstern are Dead,*[1] Marowitz's *Hamlet,*[2] Bernard Kops's *Hamlet of Stepney Green,*[3] St. John Hankin's *New Wing at Elsinore.*[4] The present play *Goodnight Desdemona (Good Morning Juliet)*[5] by Ann-Marie MacDonald is the Canadian/Feminist contribution to this playful study of Shakespeare through another play.

The director of the play Banuta Rubess, in her introduction to the play says:

> For myself, the greatest pleasure of the piece is its scope—in terms of content, in terms of theatricality, and ultimately, in terms of the place it gives to women. The women of *Goodnight Desdemona* are always pushing the piece forward, threatening, seducing, giving up, rallying, stabbing, kissing, embracing, thinking. Their astounding variety seems logical considering the woman who created them. After all, Ann-Marie MacDonald is herself a feminist. (9)

It has been mentioned at the beginning of the text that "the text combines prose and blank verse; text in blank verse is indented. Direct quotes from Shakespeare are set in Zapt chancery Italic." (4) Also "the play proceeds in a hermetic landscape of thought, setting and character." (8) "The real story happens in the zone of the unconscious mind" and "Desdemona and Juliet are archetypes." (8) Obviously a straightforward comment on this hilarious re-visioning of Shakespeare's tragedies as comedies would be simplistic. Essentially, it remains a brilliant theatrical *tour de force*—a contemporary post-Jungian feminist interpretation of Desdemona and Juliet. Needless to say, a good knowledge of the original plays is necessary to appreciate the mischievous mis-re-interpretations of passages that are well known. There are, in fact, more than thirty quotations from Shakespeare. What has become of these quotes alone can form an independent study of *Goodnight Desdemona (Good Morning, Juliet)*. However the restricted comment must confine itself to argue the feminist thrust.

II

Good old Ruskin in his famous essay "Of Queen's Gardens" argued that the heroines of Shakespeare are all good and great (with rare exceptions like Goneril, Regan, Lady Macbeth etc.) and that they saved the blundering men from disaster. This romantic-chivalrous attitude is passe and naive and will not do in this Age of Feminism.

Goodnight Desdemona (Good Morning Juliet) is essentially an academic play. The scene shifts to another "Queen's Gardens"—Constance Ledbelly's office at Queen's University, Kingston, Canada. It is through Constance's consciousness, her Ph.D. work, her ghost-writing, her hunt for "Sources," her being exploited by Professor Night, her being ditched by him, her own voyage of self-discovery and finding that she is seeking her own "source"—all these are portrayed with devastating and monstrous cleverness in the play by Ann-Marie MacDonald, "the feminist." Before we look at the changed characters of Desdemona and Juliet as portrayed here, it is necessary to take notice of the framework itself. Professor Claude Night has been exploiting Constance constantly and with unvarying consistency and is making her do his work—ghost writing for him—and just when she is hoping that he will help her to a better University position finds that he himself is leaving for Oxford along with a student Ramor a, obviously "metal more attractive"! She learns that "when lovely woman stoops to folly" and that "men betray," Desdemona in the play after she has became Constance's friend (calls her "Con" affectionately) advises her to "learn to kill" (37) and when Con, who has been conned refuses, Desdemona calls it her "sole deficiency" (37) and says: "An errant woman that would live along, no husband there, her honour to defend, must study to be bloody." (37) Constance has admired Professor Night too long to hate him for what he has done but she says she "resents" what he has done and Desdemona calls him "a false foe" and "a thief." (40) Constance confesses to her:

> I've slaved for years to get my doctorate,
> but in a field like mine that's so well trod,
> you run the risk of contradicting men
> who've risen to the rank of sacred cow,
> and dying on the horns of those who rule
> the pasture with an iron cud.
> Not that I'm some kind of feminist.
> I shave my legs and I get nervous in a crowd—
> it's just that. . . . I was labelled as a crackpot,
> by the sacred herd of Academie. (41)

One suspects that Ann-Marie MacDonald, in her brilliant spoof, does not spare even feminism itself and pokes fun at it. That is what makes the play a devastating tract with internal comments. Despite the light bantering tone and the most enjoyable comic context, Desdemona is outraged that a constant woman like Constance should be taken for a ride by an inconstant man. In a mock-serious academic scholarly language, Desdemona the "feminist" bursts forth:

Desdemona: Ten years of ghostly writing for a thief? Thy mind hath proved a cornucopia, to slake the glutton, sloth, and he has cooked his stolen feast on thy Promethean heat.

Constance: You really think so?

Desdemona: Ay! thou wast in thrall; ten years an inky slave in paper chains! (40)

and advises Constance:

> Gird thou thy trembling loins
> and slay Professor Night! (41)

Despite the parody, this gives some idea about the new feminist Desdemona as conceived by Ann-Marie MacDonald and this introduction serves to take a further look at her Desdemona. Act II concerns itself with the Desdemona aspect of the play and Act III moves on to Juliet.

III

Desdemona welcomes Constance with the words "Con, thou art an amazon." (35)

> And ruled by mighty Queens, a race of amazons who brook no men. (34)

and Constance confesses:

> My Queens have charged me with a fearful task. I must find out my true identity and then discover who the author be. (34)

This is the theme of the play. However, the point is that Desdemona is quite an "amazon" in this play and a "feminist." When Constance exposes the black plot of Iago, Desdemona takes to her but the ironic twist is that so does Othello! Iago, the born villain, seizes this opportunity and in a savage ironic reversal of the original, he incenses Desdemona against the Moor. She is made to suspect that Othello is having an affair with Constance. The plot gets thicker and more and more hilariously comic and there is an "inside" comment given to Constance herself in an "aside":

> I've wrecked a masterpiece. I've ruined the play.
> I've turned Shakespeare's "Othello" to a farce. (30)

The stage direction of Act II, Scene 1 reads "Othello and Iago reprise the end of the 'Handkerchief Scene.' Desdemona's 'strawberry spotted' handkerchief hangs out the back of Iago's house" (29) and Constance "plucks the handkerchief from Iago's house and gives it to Othello." (30) Thus it is that the villain is exposed and female tragedy is averted by a "feminist" assistant professor of English at Queen's University! Constance is the saviour of Desdemona and makes Desdemona assert: "And we be women; not mice." (37) Iago is punished by Othello to bear "two buckets of filth on a yoke." However, Iago the consummate villain with a motive full of malignity towards Constance reveals in a sort of soliloquy that he will be revenged by poisoning the mind of Desdemona:

> I'll tell her Constance is a spy and whore
> would skewer state and marriage on the same cabob
> Thus I blind and train by falcon for the job. (39)

The "diabolic intellect" is in full swing. Constance is supposed to have bewitched Othello. In this play—a parody—an ironic inversion is effected effectively and Desdemona's anger is aroused. She declares:

> I'll split her head upon a pike for daws to peck at.
> Thou wilt instruct me in the manly work
> of sword-play; doubtless she is expert, there
> for all her lack-a-liver timid show. (45-46)

Desdemona asks Iago "How shall I kill her, Iago?" and "Iago hands Desdemona the pillow." (52) A total reversal of the situation from the original, which is also quoted at the beginning of the play where Iago advises Othello: "Strangle her in bed, even the bed she hath, contaminated." (18) At this point it is necessary to turn to the Introduction by the director regarding the origin of this brilliant parody:

> It began with a joke. On a tour of England in 1985 with *This is for Your Anna* (a previous work by Ann-Marie MacDonald) Ann-Marie MacDonald crammed a pillow on my face and with great hilarity pronounced 'Goodnight, Desdemona!' Something snapped, a clear sound pervaded the air, and a masterpiece was born. (7)

The feminist twist is evident when the famous dialogue between Othello and Iago is re-written as the dialogue between Desdemona and Iago. Compare the two versions:

Othello: Indeed? Ay indeed!
Discern'st thou ought in that?
Is he not honest?
Iago: Honest, My Lord?
Othello: Honest? Ay, honest.
Iago: My lord for ought I know.
Othello: What dost thou think?
Iago: Think, my lord?
Othello: Think, my lord:
By heaven, thou echoest. . . .
If thou dost love me, show me thy thought.
Iago: My Lord, you know I love you. (17)

Now, the second version:

Desdemona: Indeed, Ay, indeed,
Discern'st thou ought in that?
Is she not honest?
Iago: Honest, madam?
Desdemona: Honest, aye, honest.
Iago: For what I know.
Desdemona: What dost thou think?
Iago: Think, my lady?
Desdemona: Think, my lady?
By heaven, thou echoest me.
Thou dost mean something.
If thou dost love me, show me thy thought
Iago: M'lady you know I love you. (43)

Othello questioning about Cassio and Desdemona questioning about Constance, through the clever reversal of the situation, the defence of Desdemona is achieved and Othello, the macho male chauvinist is exposed. Instances can be multiplied but since "brevity is the soul of wit" and the play itself is very witty, it is time to move on to Act III, the re-visioning of *Romeo and Juliet.* However before that the ending of Act II:

Desdemona: How shall I kill her Iago?
(Iago hands Desdemona the pillow) (52)

Thus the "tragedy of the handkerchief" becomes the comedy of the hanky and the pillow! There is even a pillow fight between Desdemona and Juliet: "Juliet hits Desdemona with the pillow, but Desdemona disarms her easily and knocks her flying" (80) which brings us to the *Good Morning Juliet* part of the play.

IV

The parody continues and Constance disguises herself as a man and calls herself Constantine, a la Viola-Cesario in *Twelfth Night*. However the "complications" are of a different nature in this unromantic, feminist, re-working where homosexuality, lesbianism, and transvestite themes figure. Shakespeare's "Bawdy" takes on post-women's lib turn. For example, the stage direction, "Lewd Renaissance gestures and laughter throughout the following dreadful jokes" (54) is followed by the dialogue:

Mercutio: When that her kinsfolk 'venge her maidenhead!
Tybalt: She'd never known who'd had her maidenhead.
For I would pass as quickly through the wench,
as my fruit so green, would pass through me! (54)

Romeo himself is different from legendary archetypal romantic lover. He is attracted to Constance as Constantine, the 'Greek boy' (which is very different from the way Olivia falls in love with Viola as Cesario in *Twelfth Night*). Even at the time of the wedding feast, he says:

If only Constantine were here tonight:
this feast were better borne in the light of him. (61)

The modern Italian Romeo that he is, he combines the old and new. He tells Juliet:

There's some fun going forward at the
gondolier: the fellows and I are getting
up a Cock-fight, followed by a bear-baiting,
then hie us to a public hanging in the piazza,

> there to take our noon-day meal. (aside)
> I mean to find a lovely Greek boy,
> Constantine, or die. (56)

Romeo "embraces Constance warmly taking her off-guard" and declares:

> Speak not of Juliet, it's thee I love . . .
> O Constantine, O emperor of my heart (62)

The sheer hilarity of the writing of Ann-Marie MacDonald is evident throughout:

Constance: I am not that kind of boy.
Romeo: What kind of boy?
Constance: The kind that can just hop right
into bed with any Tom or Dick or . . .
Romeo.
Romeo: Where be these rivals, Tom and Dick? (63)

The fun increases when we find that Juliet is attracted to Constance as Constantine and declares in an "aside":

> Hail, Roman Cupid that hath heard my cries,
> and sent Greek Eros to benight mine eyes! (64)

Juliet 'takes Constance's hand and does not release it' (64). The comic romp continues when both Romeo and Juliet are in love, not with each other but with Constance-Constantine! Romeo perceives Juliet's interest in Constantine and wants to win his love by becoming a transvestite. He asserts:

> I'll wear a woman's gown until I die,
> sith it's piece of skirt that likes his eye! (66)

Not to be outdone, Juliet in turn dresses herself in Romeo's clothing and the transvestitism continues. The following dialogue is one of the most hilarious in the whole play:

Juliet: Indeed. Thou art a deviant of Greece.
O Constantine! O wherefore art
thou bent?
Constance: Shshsh! Good Heavens, keep your

voice down please:

Juliet: Deny thy preference and refuse thy sex:
or, if thou wilt not, be but sworn my love,
and henceforth never will I be a girl.

Constance: I'm not . . . a deviant, for heaven's sake.

Juliet: Not deviant? Art thou then a timid virgin?
Dear boy, I envy thy bliss to come.

Constance: I may be a celibate but I'm not exactly a virgin.

Juliet: Tut, boyish bluster.
Hast thou tasted woman?

Constance: No!

Juliet: Then are thy vestal senses all intact.
O let Juliet initiate thy budding
taste of woman's dewy rose. (69)

V

Ann-Marie MacDonald's *Goodnight Desdemona (Good Morning Juliet)* is one of the most remarkable plays to have come out in recent years. It has elements of the "Theatre of the Absurd" also, and it is quite possible to consider it under that genre as well. Ann-Marie is a brilliant parodist and just one more example should bring this discussion to a close. One of the famous soliloquies of Hamlet assumes this form:

> O, what would Desdemona do to Claude
> had she the motive and the cue for passion
> that I have? She would drown all Queen's with blood
> and cleave Claude Night's two typing fingers from
> his guilty hands. She'd wrap them in a box
> of choc'lates and present them to Ramona.
> She'd kill him in cold blood and in blank verse
> then smear the ivied walls in scarlet letters
> spelling "thief"! (49)

Shakespeare's name itself comes in for a pun:

Constance: Have you known God to be called Shakespeare?

Desdemona: Shake Spear? He might be a pagan God of War. (36)

Even Shakespeare's own epitaph is pronounced by Desdemona: "Blessed be the man that spares these stones. And cursed be he that moves by bones. William." (82) It is said right at the beginning of the play in a Note: "The bard is immanent and beyond thanks." (4) Typical of the play *Goodnight Desdemona (Good Morning Juliet)*. Not since Tom Stoppard's *Rosencrantz and Guildenstern are Dead* has there been such a brilliant "revisioning" of Shakespeare.

NOTES

1. Tom Stoppard, *Rosencrantz and Guildenstern are Dead* (London: Faber and Faber, 1967).
2. Charles Marowitz, *The Marowitz Hamlet* (Penguin).
3. Bernard Kops, "The Hamlet of Stepney Green," *Three Plays* (Penguin).
4. St. John Hankin, "The New Wing at Elsinore," *The Drama Bedside Book*, ed. H.F. Rubinstein and J.C. Trewin (London, Victor Gollancz, 1966), pp. 351-58.
5. Ann-Marie MacDonald, *Goodnight Desdemona (Good Morning Juliet* (Toronto: Coach House Press, 1990).

Woman as a Victim of Marriage: Erika Ritter's *Automatic Pilot*

Mary Jane Edwards, writing about women's writing in Canada says:

> From the beginning of Canadian Literature in English, many women have written poetry, fiction, and drama, including Frances Brooke, the author of *The History of Emily Montague* (1769), the work usually called the first Canadian novel. Most have written from a recognizably female point of view in that they have created main characters who are women, and they have explored subjects of particular interest to women. Some of them have used their creative writing to develop specifically feminist ideas. A high proportion of them has been remarkably successful. One woman who exemplified all these traits was Lucy Maud Montgomery, the author of *Anne of Green Gables* (1908), the work which Mavis Gallant echoed in the title of her collection of short stories, *My Heart is Broken* (1964), and which the liberated Sarah Porlock gave away with regret in Marian Engel's *No Clouds of Glory* (1968). It was Marian Engel who suggested that one reason why women frequently tried to earn their living by writing was that it was the cheapest of the arts and could be done at home.[1]

Margaret Atwood, in her seminal work *Survival*, speaks of 'Victim Positions'. This is a suitable framework to analyze woman as victim in Erika Ritter's plays, especially her *Automatic Pilot*.[2]

Erika Ritter was a student of McGill University, Montreal, and graduated in drama in 1968. Later on, she was a 'writer-in-residence' at Concordia University, again at Montreal. Her first play *A Visitor from Charleston* was staged in 1974. Her second play *The Splits* was a popular success both at Toronto Free Theatre and Actors' Theatre at Louisville in 1978. This was followed by her third play, *Automatic Pilot* which opened in January 1980 at Toronto's Adelaide Court, and reopened in the summer for an extended run, subsequently playing in seven regional theatres from Thundur Bay to Victoria. It was so successful thai when the play won the Chalmes Award for 1980, Ritter split the $ 5000 cash prize with director William Lane, explaining that 'Marriage is a comparatively trivial undertaking beside finding a good director'. This is a characteristic statement by Ritter because all her plays centre round marriage—particularly the failure in marriage. She gives an apparently comic twist to her plays. Nevertheless, she deals seriously with the woman as a victim of marriage. The woman is victimized by her husband's inadequacies. There is a certain element of duality, resulting in a dilemma: 'To marry or not to marry, that is the question! The choice is a difficult one because in marriage—even in a bad marriage—there is a sense of security. But in single solitude, however much the person may love independence, it is a painful path to follow. More often than not, there is not only insecurity but also confusing codes of sexual behaviour, especially when the woman is a career woman with a job. Whether she is a writer or a performer, certain complications set in. In *Automatic Pilot*, this marital problem is discussed, though in a comic context. Another 'feminist' playwright from Canada, Ann-Marie MacDonald, it may be remembered, has turned Shakespeare's Desdemona and Juliet into feminists in her comic re-working of *Othello* and *Romeo and Juliet*.

In Erika Ritter's first play *A Visitor from Charleston*, Eva the main character experiences emotional disturbances in her life because of an actor ex-boyfriend and a 'would-be' novelist, an ex-husband. In her second play *The Splits*, Megan, who is a script-writer, tries to 'Split' from all dependencies which diminish her as a human being. The problem is with her ex-husband who exploits her and the producers who want to alter her serious drama. Her fourth play *The Passing Scene*, produced in the Tarragon theatre in 1982, deals with the shaky marriage of a pair of journalists. Thus, it is seen from the above discussion that the central theme of Erika Ritter in her plays is the breakdown of marriage and the woman, who is the protagonist, is seen as the 'victim'. A word about the title 'Automatic Pilot'. The syndrome refers to the switch that is pulled whenever she can't face reality head-on.

The play has only four characters—Charlie 30, Alan her husband, who is also 30 and her two lovers Gene who is 23 and Nick who is 35. There is an in-built contrast between the two lovers. Nick is a macho man whereas Gene is delicate. Her husband Alan moves in a twilight zone—a complex homosexual-heterosexual character. The marital problem of Charlie is more complicated than the problems of other women of Ritter. If it is difficult to live with a man who leaves her for another woman, it is even more difficult if he leaves for another man. It is a double affront to her womanhood and in her state of mind to prove to herself that she is a proper woman, she takes on lovers who appreciate her for what she is—an attractive woman. The play in Two Acts has 8 scenes in Act I, and 5 scenes in Act 2. The 'time' of the play is the absolute present as the action takes place in the 1960s, 70s and 80s. The place is Toronto. Many scenes are laid in the club called 'Canada Goose'. The language of the play is absolutely uninhibited as many four-letter words are used quite freely. It is a bit surprising, at least for the present writer, that a woman playwright is doing this. However, why not? In this twenty-first century, we have gone beyond postmodernism, postcolonialism and perhaps post-feminism and post women's lib. The language of the play is also 'quite liberated'. Drama has to use the spoken language reflecting the characters that are being portrayed. Here, Charlie uses the language of a modern North American, whether of the U.S. or Canada. It is perhaps significant that Charlie is a woman in the play though generally the name is associated with a man. She is full of paradoxes psychologically and as a performer on the stage she wears on male clothing to perform a self-deprecating comedy routine that presents her as unfeminine and unattractive as a transvestite. On the other hand, in her need to revenge her husband's homosexual choice, she becomes almost schizophrenically a nymphomaniac. Charlie seems able to operate only in the extreme. She is either monogamous or promiscuous. She seems to entertain a need to destroy herself and her boyfriend, Nick helps her in this and in keeping with the outspokenness of the language of the play, he is described 'a bastard but refreshingly honest about it'. At the risk of being risqué, the following remark of Charlie, talking about being in bed with men may be quoted:

> A session with your average older man is like a screening of *The Sorrow and the Pity*. Only longer and sadder. You nod off two or three times and wake up, and he's STILL at it. 'I almost came that time', he says. Eventually, you start trying to outfox him, right? 'You came' you tell him. 'You definitely came. It's just been so long you've forgotten what it's like. But that was it. Trust me. Now, can we get some sleep?'
>
> But the real bitch about younger men is how goddaman earnest they are. One roll in the hay, and they're ready to move in—provided you're willing to help them with the algebra. (376)

The technical aspect of the play indeed is very interesting in so far as there are long speeches given to Charlie, making this a kind of 'one woman play'. The 'one woman play' is a type of 'Monologue' which is a unique stage performance which has been particularly the forte of actresses like Cecelia Loftus in England, Beatrice Herford and Ruth Draper in the United States and Beverley Simon in Canada.

One of the most promising actresses who writes her own plays is Connie Clark in Yale whose performances were witnessed by the present writer, followed by a discussion of her art. Since *Automatic Pilot* is gynocentric in nature, the three men in the play are marginalized. If John Osborne's *Look Back in Anger* was described as 'a one-man play', this play could be described as 'a one-woman play'. In fact, the play opens with Charlie speaking to the audience directly, being almost a stage manager (a sort of a 'Sutradhara' in Sanskrit drama). This technique has been adapted by Tennessee Williams in his *The Glass Menagerie* where Tom is both a character in the play as well as the chorus commentator outside the play. Just a few lines from the beginning of the play may be quoted here to indicate the 'mise en scene':

> Lights come up on the area of the stage designated as *The Canada Goose*, a comedy club, suggested by a mike on a stand and a spotlight. Charlie, dressed simply in a blouse and jeans, and without her glasses, stands nervously at the mike, speaking awkwardly into it without daring to remove it from the stand.
>
> Charlie to the Audience: I decided to try my luck as New Talent tonight, because at my age, it's an accomplishment to appear as new anything. . . . Actually, I'm accustomed to making a fool of myself. In real life, I'm the head writer for a soap opera. (353)

Throughout the play, there is a change of place and time, though we do return to the 'Canada Goose' later on. The passage of time is indicated in the various scenes in Stage Directions like 'A couple of weeks later'; 'A few days later'; 'Two days later'; 'A few hours later'; 'A day or two later'; 'Four weeks later'; 'The next morning'; 'Some weeks later' etc. The stage direction also indicates Charlie's state of mind. For example, 'Lights come up Charlie on the phone in her apartment. There are a couple of empty wine bottles beside her and she has a glass in her hand. She is drunk, but not inarticulate. A bouquet of roses is bundled conspicuously in a wastebasket'. (365) The next scene is 'A few hours later. Lights up in Charlie's apartment. The scene is unchanged except for an added empty bottle or two'. (366) The play ends with another long speech by Charlie, similar to the one with which the play started. It is relevant to invoke Mary Jane Edwards again by way of summing up women's writing in Canada"

> Contemporary Canadian women have continued the traditions of their predecessors. During the 1970s, women were especially prominent in fiction, as the names of Margaret Atwood, Marian Engel, Mavis Gallant, Margaret Gibson, Margaret Laurence, and Alice Munro suggest. With few exceptions, the chief characters in

> the poems, novels, and plays of contemporary women writers were women. . . . Many Canadian women dealt with subjects, sometimes with a specifically feminist stance, that were of particular importance to them and their sisters. . . . Above all, Canadian women writers continued to be remarkably successful, as the career of Margaret Atwood showed most dramatically in the 1970s.[3]

NOTES

1. Erika Ritter, *Automatic Pilot*, *Modern Canadian Plays* (rev. ed.) ed. Jerry Wasserman (Vancouver: Talon Books, 1986), pp. 351-77.
2. Paul Denham and Mary Jane Edwards, "Introduction," *Canadian Literature in the 70s* (Toronto: Holt, Rinehart and Winston, 1980), p. xix.
3. *Ibid.*, pp. xix-xx.

Seven Ages of a Woman: Beverley Simon's *Preparing*

All the world's stage,
And all the men and women merely players:
They have their exits and their entrances;
And one man in his time plays many parts,
His acts being seven ages.

Shakespeare, *As You Like It*, Act II, Sc. 7

Preparing by Beverley Simons[1] is a remarkable one-act, one-person play which spans the entire life of an archetypal woman in seven stages—seven ages. It is meant for a virtuoso performance by a great actress, with many exits and entrances, playing many parts from a schoolgirl to the final exit, as a shrouded corpse. The social concern of Beverley Simons was highlighted when her earlier play *Crabdance* was described as "a complex, difficult symbolic work": "It has been read as a statement about the need for ritual and belief in a secularized modern world; a psychological drama about relationships between men and women; and as a social play about the role of consumerism in reducing every human relation to that between a salesman and his client." (96) *Preparing* is no less complex as it compresses and epitomizes the whole life-span of a woman into about an hour's presentation on the stage. "It also combines the metaphysical, the psychological and the social. In a monologue that uses dance and mime, Jeannie acts out the various ages and social roles of women." (97)

The "Monologue" is a unique form of stage presentation which has been exploited to the full by Beverley Simons in this play which was produced in Simon Fraser University in Vancouver in 1973. Speaking about this particular art form, it must be noted:

> The monologue is a special form of acting, a dramatic composition for a single performer, evoking other characters upon the stage. Over the years of theatre history there have been many practitioners: Cecelia Loftus in England, Beatrice Herford in the United States. . . . But no one before Ruth Draper, had such mastery, such range or such complete independence of all aids; none were exclusively their own playwright. She was the greatest exponent of this form of theatre art.[2]

Three things that are particularly interesting to the present writer about *Preparing* are: (1) It contains in the Canadian context a particular theatre form which seems to have been the forte of women—in England as well as in the United States. (2) It uses the central metaphor of theatre "with its rehearsals, masks, costumes, and rituals" (97) to represent existence—life itself. (3) Beverley Simons has travelled in the Far East and she has a drama called *Leela Means to Play* with all the ramifications of the Indian word "Leela." Indeed the whole of life is nothing but a "leela" in the Indian philosophical sense. *Preparing* is also a woman's leela with many parts to play until the final exit. After all, "All the world's a stage" and the whole of life is but an illusion—play-acting. That is why the first stage direction itself of *Preparing*, prepares us for this vision of life:

> *Preparing* belongs to the actress. It could be done anywhere without special lighting: she could simply enter at the beginning and leave when she's finished, carrying the box under her arm. The shifts of emotion and time happen through her. (83)

It is most significant that "the first object Jeannie takes from her box is the mirror" (84)—the symbol of illusion. If this is indicated in the very first stage-direction, it is no accident that it is re-inforced in the very last stage-direction: "Jeannie goes to the mirror and looks into it. She places the mirror face down back into the box, then slowly walks to stage centre. With a simple gesture she covers her face and head with a shawl. The dress, hanging loose, has become a shroud." (96) Thus, from the beginning to the end, life is reflected upon as a reflection in a mirror—a mere illusion, a "leela." Indeed the whole world is an illusion according to Advaita philosophy: "Vishwam darpana drishyamana nagari."[3] An individual human life—woman's life here—is the symbol of the lives of all women, everywhere, thus bestowing a universal significance to the particular Canadian woman's—Jeannie's—acting out the ages of a woman.

The first "age" of Jeannie is as a young girl "in early teens." *Preparing* begins with the brash rebellion of early teens. As Jeannie talks, adjusts her dress, hair and make-up, she matures." (83)

She enters her second age—stage of "Preparing"—Her "maturing" consists of dreams of glamour and romantic illusions. She is conscious of her physical plainness and imagines herself as a Nordic princess or an Arabian Nights seductress, "smelling of figs and pomegranates" or as the "daughter of Egyptian royalty." (85) She resents her bourgeois birth and upbringing—debunks her parents:

> "Cette bouteille de vin n'est pas assez bien." Shit! My father can no more tell the difference between one wine and another than my mother can identify French perfumes. But they're both authorities on everything. (87)

This social debunking and protest seems to have prompted her to become a stripper by profession, "Jeannie applies heavy blots of make-up to her forehead, chin, nose, spots of red on her cheeks, a Cupid's bow mouth" (87) and "as in a strip, Jeannie has rhythmically unwound her sash, which she uses erotically." (88) This is her Third Act! Her fourth age consists of her entering the matrimonial stage, "She pulls her white smock over her head again. No longer a uniform, it becomes her wedding gown." (98) Pregnancy follows marriage and "Aware of the changes in her body, her belt rises as her belly expands with pregnancy. . . . The maternity dress has become a hospital robe." (88-89) The fifth stage is the divorced state: "Jeannie takes off her wedding ring and drops it into the box." (92) The sixth stage is that of the hard-headed business woman bent on a successful career. Naturally, the stage props change, "From the box she lifts the platinum or blonde wig and pulls it over her hair. Then she takes out her dark coloured glasses. . . . There is now a sophisticated hardness. . . . She has aged. . . . Her voice has deepened." (93) This sixth stage perhaps represents the modern feminist woman who has taken her official place in society and is the emergent independent committee and conference woman. As she says: "Yes, I'm on the boards of the Art Gallery, the Theatre, the Symphony, the Opera as well as the countless societies for human reform. . . . I believe in running the arts like a business. . . . Miniatures may be back this season. I promote economy in the Arts." (94) This picture of the opinionated, sententious, officious successful "public" woman corresponds to the fifth age of a man in Jacques's speech:

> The justice,
> In fair round belly, with good capon lin'd
> With eyes serene, and beard of formal cut,
> Full of wise saws and modern instances,
> And so he plays his part.[4]

The modern archetypal woman acts her age—pun intended! "She pulls out the perfume flask which now contains whisky and a bottle of pills. She shakes several pills into her hand and washes them down." (94) A long way from Shakespeare's women—or men!—but the contemporary "surge in feminism" is at work in this significant play by Beverley Simons and "the last scene of all" in Shakespeare of "second childishness and mere oblivion" gives place to a stage where Jeannie, though she "ages as she speaks" and "her voice is thin," her body is still "tough and straight." (95) When her seventh stage has arrived and she goes out with a bang by boasting that "They're naming a new theatre after me" (95) and using the brave new language of a no-nonsense feminist says: "Fuck'em all. I've never cared for establishments or institutions, but it seems I've spawned one.

Hurry, old woman, you're always late. For what?" (96) This last speech of Jeannie in *Preparing* where she speaks of "Preparing for the future" (96) leads to the last sentence of the stage-direction with which the play ends: "Her Preparing is over." Yes, her "leela" is over in this world and she is ready for her "future." Beverley Simon's *Preparing* prepares us for an extraordinary theatrical experience of a one-woman theatre which is equally successful both as a modern, very contemporary portrayal of a feminist sensibility as well as a technical tour de force.

NOTES

1. Beverley Simons, "Preparing," *Canadian Literature in the 70s*, ed. Paul Denham and Mary Jane Edwards (Toronto: Holt, Rinehart and Winston of Canada, 1980), pp. 82-97.
2. *The Letters of Ruth Draper 1920-1956, a Self Portrait of a Great Actress*, Foreword by Sir John Gielgud, ed. with narrative notes by Neilla Warren (New York: Charles Scribner's, 1979), p. 14.
3. Adi Shankaracharya, *Dakshinamurthy Stotram*, Stanza 1, Line 1.
4. Shakespeare, *As You Like It*, Act II, Sc. 7.

A Document of Women in French Canadian Society: Michel Tremblay's *The Impromptu of Outremont*

Michel Tremblay's *The Impromptu of Outremont* can be described as a French-Canadian social document. It is a remarkably powerful play about the changing society and values in Quebec and the play discusses the old traditional bourgeois values in relation to the onset of the working class pop culture at various levels—of language, of literature, of music and the social institution of marriage in relation to four sisters from Montreal. In fact, all the four characters in the play are women. It is, in a manner of speaking, a play of ideas—a play that stimulates thinking on the part of the readers/audience. The nature of the 'conflict' in the play is in the nature of a clash of ideas and ideals, of priorities and preferences. It is primarily a 'discussion drama' and so there is very little 'action' but only a great deal of talk—vigorous, provocative, argumentative, even abusive talk—where four sisters tear each other to bits in mutual recriminations though the occasion is the birthday of one of the sisters, Lorraine, who is forty and it is supposed to be a day on which 'truce' is declared. The play presents the "action"—such as it is—in one continuous movement, the Second Act following the First in a continuity and it is remarkable that the time taken for the presentation of the play is the same as the time taken 'in the play' for the characters to argue and tear each other apart. The locale is 'Outremont' in Montreal and the Westmont society is contrasted with the working area of East Montreal. The play is marked by a remarkable unity of time as has been pointed out and to help this, there are only four characters—the four Beaugrand sisters—Fernande who is 50, Yvette, 46, Lorraine, 43, and Lucille, whose birthday it is, is 40. On these special occasions when the four sisters meet, it is an 'impromptu' when they are at each others' throats in spite of the so-called 'truce' and since they meet in the 'living room of a bourgeois home in Outremont,' the play is called *The Impromptu of Outremont.* Now let us briefly examine how it is a social comment on the French-Canadian women in Montreal society.

II

It is perhaps best to begin with a reference to the theatre where Tremblay is contrasting the old Romantic-Nostalgic theatre with the modern one. Fernande, who is the representative of the good old Outremont culture, lashes out at the so-called modern theatre of which Tremblay himself is one of the major dramatists if not the new dramatist:

> I've ridden on the wings of the theatre for almost twenty years, from the Venice of the Doges to the bloody England of Elizabeth, from la noble France to Spain, proud and sombre! And all I saw was admirable! All that I heard was beautiful! And when the curtain fell after those fleeting hours of boundless happiness, my heart would stop, my life held captive behind the red velvet curtain. And I'd nourish myself for days on the substance of what had been granted me! But today, for the most part, especially in the so-called 'new culture,' the curtain doesn't even exist. Fini, the sacred mystery! Fini, the voyage of initiation! You walk into a theatre and the set hits you in the face! If the actors aren't there already waiting for you, mumbling their text or staring out at you, as if the characters in a play could see you! Yet, you having paid to be looked at, you've paid to look! And when the . . . play begins, they provoke you, insult you, cover you in filth. . . . Nothing is too vile, nothing too ugly, too low. The poor spectator is lured into the theatre and trapped there like a rat. They've even done away with intermission. And they shout in your face using language that would make your hair stand on end. (73-74)

The rather long passage has been quoted here to show two things. First, it sets down in unmistakable terms the nostalgic mood that characterizes Fernande who represents the old Outremont culture of the elite of French Canada—of Montreal in particular—and secondly Michel Tremblay, a playwright of the 'new culture' knows how to project the opposite point of view. In every aspect of art, not only in the theatre, is the new trend present and the opposite point of view to this is represented too:

> Oh Fernande, are you going to pontificate again on the pollution of joual verses the natural undulation of la langue francaise? You should be thankful the curtain is gone. Wouldn't it be cruel of theatre people to tantalize you, to keep you in suspense, put you into a trance, give you stage fright, only to hand you an East Montreal kitchen! You'd die on the spot! (74)

This is not only a discussion about the changing drama but about Outremont versus East Montreal—Michel Tremblay himself using joual in his plays and being very much East Montreal—and it is the difference between the bourgeoisie and the working class. There is an open discussion about the use of joual and one gets the feeling—as an outsider of course who doesn't know the difference between joual and la langue francaise who has read Tremblay only in English translation—that Tremblay in this play is defensive about his own use of joual and he has made that a part of the discussion between two characters. Observe the following exchange:

Fernande: What must foreigners think when they hear our lousy French? I don't want the whole world thinking everyone here speak joual! . . .

Lucille: All we want is to be told that we're beautiful, that we speak well, that we're civilized, that we know how to suffer with dignity when misfortune befalls us. And especially, we want foreigners to think we're good enough to speak to them. What foreigners think is so much more important to us than what happens in our own country, isn't it? It's so much easier to just slip into someone else's culture than create your own. (76)

Lorraine supports her when she says: "It's true, you know, what you find beautiful, is so antiseptic, so disinfected, so sterile, you'd probably die if you caught a cold east of Boulevard St. Laurent!" (77)

In fact, through the play the social attitude of the mother—who is no more and so doesn't appear in the play—is castigated and all the blame for the failure of the four sisters is squarely laid at her door—except by Fetnande the eldest who takes after her. The mother is portrayed as an insufferable snob who had exaggerated hopes for her children but who ruined them and they are all frustrated and bitter, one way or the other. The social pretence of the mother is exposed and ridiculed when Lucille points out:

> Don't be·hypocrite! You remember perfectly well. It was one of those rainy afternoons when mother'd play bridge with the great-grandniece of Sir Wilfred Laurier, the great-granddaughter of Henri Bourassa and the last gasp in the Louis Frechette clan; she, who had no luminaries in her obscure background and who always said: "In my family tree, the celebrities aren't in the past, but in the future! I prefer the young buds to the old branches!" Our mother was the rub-of-the-mill Tremblay and so ashamed of it, she'd pretend to have a bone caught in her throat if someone asked where she came from. (12)

The only gratuitous and perhaps unnecessary remark the present writer would make at this point is that her attitude would change after the advent of the writer of this play—Michel Tremblay!

One of the beauties about this play is that there is a lot of discussion about language, literature, music and art as a part of the delineation of the social milieu. The eldest sister, Fernande, is the only one who seems to be very squeamish about the use of proper language and respectable words that are found in a good dictionary and therefore becomes the butt of ridicule for the other sisters. She is pictured as a language snob. When Yvette takes Lucille to task for using a wrong French expression, she replies: "If Fernande heard me, she would correct me and I would apologize, after having said, 'Pardon, je suis z'en forme' with the liaison in the right place. I would assume an air of contrition and put on a face of shameful defeat." (11) When Yvette uses the word "ennuyante," Lucille tries to correct her by saying, "Ennuyeuse, Yvette, ennuyeuse. . . . If Fernande heard you." (17) Interestingly enough, after Fernande makes her appearance, on the scene, she does say, "You and your petty jokes, you are so ennuyante." (31) "Upon hearing the word, ennuyante, Yvette gets up and goes to the small bookshelf and takes out a dictionary," the stage direction says, and the following dialogue ensues:

Yvette: In any case girls, one thing is settled. . . . I have just checked the dictionary. . . . Ennuyante exists in French. Listen. . . . "Ennuyant, ennuyante: adj. (Enoiant, XII century; if. ennuyer) characterized by boredom, tedium. Archaic or regional: ennuyeux."

Lucille: Wouldn't you know it regional! Will it never end? Anyway you're looking in the Petit Robert, Yvette. . . . That's no good. . . . Go look in the Larousse.

Fernande: Oh, discussing linguistics?

Lucille: Forget the dictionary, Yvette, our universal encyclopedia is at hand. (To Fernande) In your considered opinion, is ennuyant correct French?

Fernande: If I used it a moment ago, that means it's correct.

Lucille: Well, don't choke on your modesty.

Fernande: I won't, because I'm right. (33-34)

Of course she would be right because after all, she was supposed to become a great writer, just as Lorraine was supposed to become a great pianist. "Lucille traded in her tutu for knitting" and as Yvette paints out in her soliloquy "I wasn't so ready to abandon everything. I threw myself into the songs of Faure, Duparc and Debussy and I became a chanteuse de salon." (22) In fact all the four sisters are frustrated, each in her own way, though Lorraine married an Italian gardener and has many children, much to the contempt of Fernande. As a critic puts it, "The four Beaugrand sisters represent the French-Canadian intelligentsia of the Fifties whose interest in art, music, dance and literature is an adopted pose, not their life's blood."[2] In spite of her failure—she knows she has failed—Fernande continues to be a hopeless romantic never giving up her illusions and in fact, Tremblay in spite of his personal disagreement with what he makes her say, has given her some of the most eloquent passages in the play—even in translation. For example, she says:

> A work of literature lies dormant in my attic, but if release into the light of day, it could become a beacon for the new generation of writers who fumble in the dark, because for fifteen years, literature has been trampled, humiliated, butchered. . . . Literature, the real thing, must be elite; literature was invented by the elite, belongs to the elite. The masses have produced only burps, whereas the elite has raised towards heaven a clear and articulate song. That's what I believe, what I've always believed, and I should stop being ashamed of it. . . . I'll be dragged through the mud, branded reactionary, racist, fascist by all those who confuse everything. (83)

From the point of view of the discussion of social norms and values in the play, Lorraine is the foil to Fernande and she is the only one who breaks away completely from the Outremont and chooses to marry an Italian gardener and move over to the working class area. She has a positive attitude to life and has never regretted the choice she has made. The soliloquies that are given to Yvette, Fernande and Lorraine in the play show the superb dramatic art of Tremblay and in these soliloquies we really get to know the honest self-criticism and self-enquiry on the part of the characters in addition to what we understand about them in dialogue—mostly in conflict with others. What is true about literature is also true about music and Lorraine reminds Fernande, "I grew up with a passion for music, just as you did for writing, remember?" (49) Indeed "remember" is the most quintessential word in the play and every time it is used, it furthers the meaning of the play that they are all "remembering" themselves as girls and their ambitions of many, many years ago. In fact, in a special sense, it is a "memory play." Indeed, the play *The Impromptu of Outremont* opens with our hearing a record of "Dido and Aeneas" by Purcell where we hear the aria "Remember Me" and when Lucille objects to Yvette playing "Remember Me" again and again, she sarcastically suggests "something

Quebecois," (8) when exasperatedly Lucille grumbles, "Generations of singers pass but 'Remember Me' is not forgotten." (9) Yvette in her soliloquy remembers, "'Remember Me . . .' From the age of ten, I sang beneath the enraptured gaze of mother and her friends from Outremont and Westmont." (21) Lorraine, in her soliloquy, remembers, "I, too, was brought up to believe we were the cream of the society. . . . I too was led to believe by someone I hated that I had talent: But I am the lost sheep who ran away with the gardener to go raise little and curly-haired kids in the depths of the Italian ghetto." (55-56) But she has no regrets because she realizes that her life at Outremont is false and hypocritical. As she puts it,

> But Guido came into my life like a dagger thrust cleanly into the heart, making a beautiful sound that's clear, frank, precise! Freedom! An open window! Honesty! Ha! Guido's honesty, after all those years of courtesies, bows, kissing hands; of "Have-you-heard?" and "Oh, look at me!" I was carried off, like in a cloak and dagger movie, practically out of my bedroom window. My prince charming had an accent to make you shudder and nothing in his hand, but a rake, but God, he was beautiful and I loved him! I almost left Outremont on the seat of a tractor to become what sister Fernande calls common, as she holds her nose, but what I call real, laughing, singing and tapping my feet, (58)

She defends her so-called 'defection' into another social level stoutly and shows up the hypocrisy of the class represented by Fernande who wants to make out that they are the custodians of culture. The Place des Arts becomes thus a symbol though it is very real place when Fernande asks her, "What's the phobia you have for the Place des Arts?" Lorraine replies:

> Right in the middle of Stravinsky's violin concerto, I caught myself wondering how many people, HOW MANY PEOPLE, Fernande, preening and rustling in their orchestra seats, felt the least bit of respect, not to mention love, for music! And by intermission, I know this sounds pretentious, but I was at the point of believing I was the only one. (50)

Thus it is that in this powerful play, an 'impromptu' that is taking place in Outremont in Montreal the changing social scene in French Canada is discussed by four women characters.

III

Michel Tremblay seems to have involved himself very deeply in this play[3] in a personal manner. He discusses joual by making the characters refer to it constantly, as for example when Fernande is attacking it and says, "I happen to think that one doesn't have to speak joual in order to be understood, but for certain people with complexes, I suppose it's better than nothing." In fact, Tremblay makes a reference to his own famous play *Les Belles-Soeurs* which was published in 1968. Yvette says:

> When we went to see the first production of *Les Belles Soeurs* almost twenty years ago, you said: "If that's the new French-Canadian culture, those women will be our neighbours within ten years." You were already suffering from chronic paranoia! But here we are, more than ten years have gone by, and the only woman from East Montreal who can get past your front door is your cleaning lady! I don't call that fast. (68)

It is rather unusual for a playwright to mention one of his own earlier plays in a later play of his. But it has an important point to make here. This comment was very much the opinion of many critics too and as Elaine Nordocchio points out:

> For Michel Tremblay, another playwright who emerged during this time, the Quebec question was very much a linguistic and economic one. Tremblay was the first dramatist, not only to write consistently in *joual* but also to deal explicitly with the sorry state of the Quebec working class. His plays succeeded in establishing that the worker's problems and language were worthy of official and popular respect and recognition. When *Les Belles-Soeurs* was first produced at the Theatre du Rideau Vort in 1968, Tremblay's stylized use of working-class French was an immediate subject of debate. Never before had there been a play that used joutal so exclu-

> sively and that so clearly and aggressively presented life on the wrong side of the tracks in Montreal.
>
> The language was called 'vulgar' by those who reacted negatively to the crude terms used in the play and 'disgraceful' by those who claimed that working-class language was suitable for the street but not for the stage. Others felt that it was time someone dealt with the linguistic and social realities of the working class in Quebec. Regardless of their personal language preferences, everyone agreed that Tremblay's vibrant use of joual and his recreation of its squalid context established a new image of Quebecois and the common linguistic bound that unites many of them. Joual soon came to be commonplace in Quebec theatre as well as in Quebecois novels and poetry.[4]

This is the reason why Tremblay brings up a reference to his earlier play in *Impromptu* as the subject matter of the play is social distinctions, including language.[5] The play *The Impromptu of Outremont* is an interesting document in the social register of Montreal. Outremont and East Montreal are the two levels that are debated and discussed by the four women characters. Outremont is discussed both as a physical place different from East Montreal as well as a 'state of mind' symbolizing a certain class of the 'elite.' For example, these two levels can be illustrated when Fernande says, "Upper Outremont is right around the corner. Two twenty five to cross Mount Royal Boulevard and Cote Sainte Catherine honestly!" (26) This is a physical locality but Lucille's reply "To get to your house, we have to go up those hills" (26) indicates a double sense of 'going up.' In fact, Fernande uses Outremont in both senses when she talks about how Outremont itself has changed:

> The great invasion has begun! First, it was the students, when the Cinema Outremont became an art house. Bus-loads of hairy-faced hippies and would-be-gypsies who occupied Bernard Street every night. . . . Then naturally, all those attractive people decided to come and live here, it was so much cleaner and quieter than the slums they came from. It's more amusing to go and dirty up your neighbour's place! Especially when he has more money. Nowa-

> days, you can't even walk your dog without being called 'bourgeois and traitor.' . . . There was a time when we did have artists in Outremont, but authentic ones, respectable ones. (66)

In fact, Lorraine debunks this snobbery of her sister when she says:

> All the kids tell me: "Oh, oh, the Belle of Outremont has surfaced again!" Well that's how it is, Fernando, when you marry the man, you marry the territory. I married the other side of Avenue du Parc; and you, on the other side of rote Sainte Catherine! The way you see it, you've gone up and I've gone down. The way I see it, I got out and you got trapped. You're so damned chic, so flashy and so shiny that, when you turn up at Place des Arts for the Tuesday night symphony, they might as well turn off the chandeliers. And your speech, it's so impeccable, every little syllable. When you go to France, they must think you're Hungarian with an M.A. in Romance languages from the University of Budapest. (46)

The final 'message' of the play is put into the mouth of Lucille: "Tolerance, Yvette. It's so much more beautiful, so much cleaner, more respectable than contempt. Your operas are the death of me and my songs drive you crazy. But we both manage to survive, don't we?" (78)

Michel Tremblay in *The Impromptu of Outremont* has given a stirring picture of French-Canadian society through analyzing the four sisters living in Montreal. It is possible to show that the opposing values about life, language and literature represented here by Fernande and Lorraine have parallels in other cultures and other literatures but this in no way takes away from the achievement of Tremblay who is perhaps the best known playwright of French Canada in recent years. To put it in the words of Elaine Nordocchio: "Tremblay sought to point out and denounce the social and cultural failings of a repressed and frustrated minority. His work also defended the right of the Quebecois to seek a better material and cultural role in the modern world."[6]

NOTES

1. Michel Tremblay, *The Impromptu of Outremont,* trans. John Van Burek (Vancouver: Talon Books, 1981).
2. *Ibid.,* the back cover.
3. Elaine F. Nordocchio in *Theatre and Politics in Modern Quebec* (The University of Alberta Press, 1986) mentions *The Impromptu of Outremont* in "Bibliography" under "French-Canadian Plays Cited" but does not include it in the section "French-Canadian Plays in Translation" (the play was published in translation in 1981). However, she mentions in her note in the beginning of "Selected Bibliography" that this bibliography lists the most important works of theatrical and socio-historical research published before 1981. No systematic attempt has been made to add the names of books and articles that appeared after that date although some outstanding works have been listed. (133) In her chapter on Michel Tremblay, Nordocchio makes a very perceptive analysis of Tremblay's plays—*Les Belles Soeurs, En Pieces Detachees, La Duchess tie Langlais, Hosanna* and some other plays. However, since there was no analysis of *The Impromptu of Outremont* the present writer felt emboldened to make the modest attempt in that direction.
4. *Ibid.,* p. 66.
5. Elaine Nordocchio summarizes the play *Les Belles Soeurs* in these words: "In *Les Belles Soeurs* (1968) we meet Germaine Lanzou, who had just won a million gold bond stamps and has invited all the other women in the neighbourhood, some of whom are related to each other, to help her stick the stamps in the appropriate books. As the evening progresses, the women become increasingly jealous of Germaine and show themselves to be anything but the 'beautiful' women the play's title refers to. They finally steal most of the stamp-filled books for themselves and flee to the sound of Germaine's desperate cries of 'My stamps! My stamps!' as all her dreams go out of the door. Ironically, of course, neither the neighbours nor poor Germaine will ever be any better off for a few gold-bond stamps cannot change one's basic socio-economic status." In the present context, this play also illustrates Tremblay's skill in delineating women characters in the social context.
6. *Ibid.,* p. 73.

Michel Tremblay's *Bonjour la Bonjour:* A Glimpse of Canadian Society in Transition

> Canadian literature may be divided into two parts, somewhat like a tree with two great roots. One root is deeply buried in the culture of France. The other is just as deeply buried in the traditions of England. One part of the Canadian literature is written in French, the other in English. But the branches of this tree are firmly Canadian. Authors and readers of each literature are gaining more and more knowledge of the other in the original or in translation.[1]

It is partly in this context of Canadian bi-lingualism that Michel Tremblay's play *Bonjour la Bonjour*[2] is chosen for a brief comment here.

William Walsh, commenting on Canadian drama says: "Drama, after its feeble non-theatrical closet existence in the nineteenth century was in modern Canada squeezed at one end by the cinema and at the other drained by the television and led only a spectral existence."[3] In spite of this remark, Michel Tremblay, who is the author of five plays[4] including the present one, is a playwright well worth discussing. *Bonjour la Bonjour* is an extremely significant play not only because of its novel technique but because it presents an interesting analysis of the French-Canadian society in transition. Indeed, it is a play originally written in French and it was first performed in French by the Compagnie des Deux Chaises at Ottawa in 1974. However, the present comment is on the English version performed in English at Toronto in 1975. The language of the play is extremely outspoken and this in itself constitutes an important aspect of the Canadian society in transition if they can accept the explosive dialogue on the stage as the London audience was ushered into a new freedom of outspokenness on the English stage with the Royal Court play, *Look Back in Anger* by John Osborne in 1956. Speaking about what Robin Matthews calls "the struggle for the voice" in Canada, he observes:

> In Quebec a high percentage of the literary artists—poets, singers, playwrights and novelists—want a unilingual independent Quebec. . . . However vaguely they take public positions, they have moved in a different way than their fellows in English Canada. They now occupy a different intellectual, cultural, ideological reality than English Canadians do. They have made certain psychological moves. They have undergone a revolution of ideas.[5]

Bonjour La Bonjour is not divided into Acts and Scenes but has 31 units which are entitled as "Solo, Duet, Trio, Quartet, Quintet and Octet" depending on how many characters are involved in the given unit. Thus we have ten "solos," five "duets," five "trios," six "quartets," one "quintet," and four "octets." The play has eight characters and they are distributed in the 31 units as mentioned. There are no stage directions except indications like "very long silence" or "very fast" and even these occur only four times in the whole play. However, it is significant that there is only one "stage direction" and it reads: "We can hear Lucienne laughing before the lights come up on her. The actress should bear in mind that in the original, Lucienne speaks French with a slight English accent as though she had lost the habit of speaking her mother tongue." (15)

Since the play *Bonjour La Bonjour* presents the changing values of the post-second war society in relation to sex, marriage and money, it is necessary to quote what some of the characters say to bring out this point. Lucienne, who is married but an adulteress, says, "I wasn't going to marry some French-Canadian turd who'd give me kids with complexes. Oh no, I was aiming higher than that, I wanted to be on the right side of the tracks, the money side, and that's where I am, dammit." (28) She is proud of the fact that she married an "Anglais." She says: "I got what I wanted. I got my Anglais. Eight years I went out with Bob before we got married." (8) In spite of her having gone out with Bob for eight years and got him, she is now "going out" with another "Bob"—Robert the painter. Serge, the young he-man of the play, who is the desired object of more than one woman in the play, doesn't mince words and right in the spirit of the play, he tells off Lucienne:

> Don't play games with me. You're supposed to be the smart one in the family, the tough one, the one who's made it. You're trying to tell me you don't know what to do? You are telling me you want to drop everything for Robert? Come on! You'd never leave all this to go hole-up in a basement with a guy who stinks of paint. I know you better than that. Look, you're married to a doctor, an Anglais on top of that, you've got a seventy thousand dollar house in Cartierville, a charming son who's started to knock up the neighbourhood girls and two lovely teenage twins who flatly refuse to learn French because their father speaks nothing but English. Now how could you leave all that, Lucienne, you love it too much. (25)

The post "Waste Land" attitude to sex, love and marriage, after the first world war and the second world war is revealed in the permissiveness that pervades this play. In fact, this Robert is no angel. As Serge points out with brutal frankness: "Oh for Chris sake, open your eyes. That's Robert's specialty, shaking up with women who could pass for his mother. Whatever happens don't take him seriously. Have your fun and when it's over, forget him. Just don't make a Greek tragedy out of it. I'm not in the mood." (24)

At this point it may not be inappropriate to go back to the subject of the language, though the problem of translation from French into English is outside the scope of the present essay. To quote Robin Matthews again:

> What is the language of English Canada? How long is it since we thought seriously about that question? Is Canadian language U.S. colloquialism? Is it CBC announcer language? Is it the language of the U.S. 'left'? Is it something else? How does the average union organizer in English Canada speak? What do Canadians expect to hear when they discuss with one another the serious questions of their polity? (157-58)

After shooting off this series of questions, he answers himself thus: "The Canadian artist who tries to convey life in Canada to the people of the country does not speak in tones of alienated, nervous, anarchistic, erotic self-indulgence. To do that is to convey the life of a tiny, neurasthenic, petty Bourgeois artistic society." (158)

In spite of this protestation, the reader of Michel Tremblay's play cannot but feel the appropriateness of some of the words used here as they seem to fit the characters of *Bonjour la Bonjour.* Indeed, Gabriel and Albertine are 'alienated,' Charlotte is 'nervous,' Serge is 'anarchistic,' Monique is 'neurasthenic,' Lucienne, Denise and Nicole are 'erotic' and 'self-indulgent.' However, it is possible to argue that this is so only in an English translation. But then Robin Matthews is talking about English in Canada, though he mentions it is the language of English Canada and not French Canada. Perhaps it is the intention of Michel Tremblay in this play to 'convey the life of a tiny, neurasthenic, petty-Bourgeois artistic society.' It doesn't seem so to the present writer as the main erotic episode in the play is the incestuous relationship of Nicole and Serge and at the end of the play, even the old man, the father, admits to having known about that 'for a long time' though everyone thought he didn't know about it. The completely uninhibited propositioning of Denise and Serge's unceremonious attitude are not exactly instances of conveying the ideal of a 'petty-Bourgeois' society through this tempestuous play.

The changing values and priorities of a society in transition are discussed in this play not only in the context of sex, marriage and money but also in terms of colonial consciousness. The attitude to France is a case in point. The attitude of Lucienne and Serge are in complete contrast to the attitude of the older generation—the pre-second world war generation—as symbolized by Gabriel who is an old man of seventy. Gabriel has a nostalgia for Paris, whereas for the younger generation represented here by Serge, it is just another place. Indeed, the first sentence of the play is "So, how did you like Europe?" (7) But Europe diminishes into France in general and Paris in particular right at the beginning of the play. For example, the question "Are European girls pretty?" (11) dissolves into the statement "We thought you might come home with a girl from Paris" (11) which is followed by the judgement, "Serge has better taste than that." (12) The fact that Serge has actually an incestuous relationship with his sister Nicole who is five years his senior has nothing to do with the judgement because for Serge as well as for Albertine who makes that statement, Paris is not what it means to old Gabriel. He is not only nostalgic about a 'Belgian girl' whom he used to know a long time ago but about Paris which he has never seen:

> Don't be afraid to tell me about Paris. Oh, I know I've never been there, but I've read a lot. I've read all about that stuff. I got the whole map of Paris right here in the old noggin. Your old man is not stupid you know. May be I've never been past Guy and Dorchester either, but at least I've read up on these things. You know the Eiffel Tower? I can tell you where it is. It's on the left bank. And Notre Dame, I know where that is too. It's on the lie de la Cite. Victor Hugo talked so much about that in his book. You know, when I was out of work during the Depression, I used to read all kinds of things. You wouldn't remember that 'cause you weren't born then, but ask Lucienne. Maupassant and all those things. I read them all. (13)

The old man with the Pre-II World War consciousness 'protesting too much' in almost a desperate bid to assert and affirm his cultural/ colonial moorings and roots becomes a foil to Serge, the 'hero' of this play, who represents the new Canadian, the uninhibited, non-sentimental, no nonsense young man of the Post-II World War. The transition in Canadian society since II World War can be understood in terms of the differing attitudes of Gabriel and Serge. Indeed, the 'colonial consciousness' in the play can be seen even in terms of such things as interior decoration and furnishings. Observe the following dialogue:

Lucienne: You can sleep in the guest room. You know it's been refurnished, eh, since you left? I got tired of the Colonial. It looked cheap. . . .
Serge: I'm the one who told you that. . . .
Lucienne: So, we bought a set of Spanish. It's gorgeous. (Silence) You're gonna love it. We put the Colonial in the basement for Bobby and his friends. (28)

The shifting of the 'Colonial' to the 'basement' represents perhaps an important aspect of the Canadian society in transition especially when we read the 'Colonial' and 'basement' as symbols. The other thing that can be read as a symbol is the reference to bridges—the bridges of Paris and the bridges of Montreal. After all, the bridge itself has been used as a symbol for quite so time.

Denise: You know those bridges? Are they right in middle of the city or all around it like the bridges in Montreal?
Serge: They're in the middle of the city. (35)

In fact, right at the end of the play, a bridge of understanding is built between Gabriel and Serge by the playwright. Thus it is possible to see how Michel Tremblay in his powerful play *Bonjour la Bonjour* has brought out a remarkable document of the Canadian society in transition since II World War.

NOTES

1. *The World Book Encyclopaedia,* vol. III (Field Enterprises Educational Corporation, 1975).
2. Michel Tremblay, *Bonjour la Bonjour,* trans. John Van Burek and Bill Glassco (Vancouver: Talon, 1975).
3. Willam Walsh, *Commonwealth Literature* (London, Oxford, New York: Oxford University Press, 1973), p. 75.
4. His plays *Hosanna*, *Les Belles Soeurs*, *Forever Yours*, *Made Lou*, *En Pieces Detachees* and *Bonjour la Bonjour* are mentioned as 'Plays in Print 1975' at the end of the play under discussion.
5. Robin Matthews, *Canadian Literature, Surrender or Revolution,* ed. Gail Dexter (Toronto: Steel Rail Educational Publishing, 1978), p. 157

Hugh MacLennan's *The Watch That Ends the Night:* An Inter-Disciplinary Approach

Hugh MacLennan begins his novel *The Watch That Ends the Night* (Toronto: Macmillan, 1958) with the sentence: "There are some stories into which the reader should be led gently and I think this may be one of them." (3) He ends the novel with an 'Epilogue' which begins with the sentence: "I could end here because my story is told. But if this has been a story into which the reader was led gently, I think it may also be one out of which he should be led factually." (370) In both these objectives the author has succeeded completely and the story itself that has been told in such a delicate web woven from the lives of three highly sensitive souls living through a difficult time in history—the 30s and the Depression years. Montreal is the *mise en scene* for the most part. Halifax, Ottawa, Toronto also do figure in the story. So do Spain, Russia and Germany to define the atmosphere against which the human drama unfolds itself. But it is Montreal that has been described with such loving care that the novel may even be taken as the story of this great city. Just one reference out of more than three dozen references to Montreal:

> It is a curious city, Montreal, and in this story I keep returning to the fact that it is. Strangers never understand its inner nature and immigrant families, even from other parts of Canada, can live here two generations without coming to know it in their bones. I am absolutely certain that Montreal is the subtlest and most intricate city in North America. With her history she could not have been otherwise and survived, for here the French, the Scotch and the English, over two centuries, have been divided on issues which ruin nations and civilizations, yet have contrived to live in outward harmony.

> This is no accident. They understand certain rules in their bones. (255)

It is in this 'subtlest and most intricate city' that three of the 'subtlest and most intricate' characters in modern literature are described, psychoanalyzed and philosophized upon. The novel is best comprehended in an inter-disciplinary approach—in terms of the political, the psychological and the philosophical levels. *The Watch That Ends the Night* is the voyage of self-exploration of three people—George who is the narrator of the story, Catherine and Jerome. There are several well-conceived minor characters like Norah Blackwell, Caroline, Sally etc. but, in the interests of focus from the inter-disciplinary approach, the three main characters are examined here briefly in terms of politics, psychology and philosophy.

II

The Watch That Ends the Night can be read as a political novel about the 30s. Spain figures so largely in the novel that Jerome's obsession about Spain, Fascism, Franco, Communism, etc., forms the very crux of the matter in the novel. The crisis in the relationship between Catherine and Jerome, the breakdown of their relationship, Norah Blackwell's affair with Jerome and her desperate bid to establish a meaningful relationship with Jerome have partly to do with the political ideology which she shares with him. The novel's 'reality' is firmly grounded in the political turmoil of the Thirties:

> I tell you, there are few people who passed through the Thirties who even dare or can recall what that time was really like or what it did to human beings. . . . There were times when, being young, I allowed myself the luxury of hope. But there was poison in the air then and I think it spread from the rotting corpses of the first war. The Thirties lie behind us like the memory of guilt and shame. (123)

George, the narrator of the story is himself a political commentator for the CBC with 'a voice a little like Roosevelt's' (278) and is immensely popular for his politically astute views. At one point in the novel the 'names and phrases of the time' (142) are given—Laskri, Keyenes, Marx, Selassie, Lenin, Ras Desta, Trotsky, Hitler, Mussolini, Goebbels, Baldwin, Chamberlain, Lansbury, Franco, Roosevelt, Dos Passos, Hemingway, etc., and is followed by the wry comment: "The 1930s was the last time in which college professors could believe themselves capable of planning the future of humanity." (142) It is interesting that the author of the novel MacLennan himself is a Professor and in many ways *The Watch That Ends the Night* is a very 'academic' novel—dealing as it does with human life at various levels lending itself for an interdisciplinary approach.

III

The Watch That Ends the Night can certainly be read as a psychological novel as the characters in the novel are analyzed with clinical precision and the motivation behind every choice and 'action' of Jerome can be discussed in terms of clinical psychology. Jerome himself is an excellent surgeon and his prowess as a healer extends beyond the operation table. He healed the patients by understanding their minds and he is aware of his own neurosis too. His mind is constantly and incessantly in conflict and so are his loyalties. His own illegitimate birth and his extremely religious upbringing by his foster parents, especially Mr. Martell the clergyman—these come into sharp conflict with his rejection of middle-class morality and indeed, he resigns his job as a surgeon at the height of his professional success to follow his political ideology in Spain and he breaks away from a perfect marital relationship with a beautiful woman Catherine and defends and teams up with another man's wife. Indeed, throughout the novel Hugh MacLennan bestows a great deal of space to expatiate upon this psychological enigma of an extraordinary man—Jerome Martell. In order to illustrate the 'psychological' dimension of the novel just one illustration—the dialogue ' tween Sally, the daughter of Jerome and Catherine and George the narrator:

> "Why does everybody stand up for him?" She said.
>
> "Everybody doesn't."
>
> "But you do. I think there is something neurotic in your whole attitude. It's all mixed up with how you feel about mummy. She loved him and you want to kid yourself you love him, too. You want to share him with her the same way you share me."
>
> I shook my head . . .
>
> "You are talking like a child," I said. "Do you think my generation invented neuroses? Do you think things in the Thirties were the same as now? Mistakes? For God's sake of course, we made them! But let me tell you something Sally. You haven't earned the right to despise your father. You may *have* that right, but by God, you have not earned it."
>
> Our eyes met and she looked away, still headstrong, considerably upset, resentful and guilty because she was. Truly I thought this girl felt guilty whenever she detected a trace of neurosis in herself and this made me smile grimly. Was neurosis the new word for sin? (47)

Indeed, throughout the novel, the three main characters, George, Jerome and Catherine are not only 'psychoanalyzing' each other but they seem to be expert psychiatrists analyzing themselves—their actions and their reactions—absolutely honestly and even ruthlessly! The question 'Was neurosis the new word for sin?' leads to the third dimension of the novel—the philosophical dimension, which indeed is the most significant one in the interdisciplinary approach to the novel.

IV

The novel *The Watch That Ends the Night* is much more than merely a good novel because of its spiritual dimension. In the case of all the three characters, who are immensely intelligent, hyper-sensitive and intensely self-critical, the thread that unites as well as separates them is their spiritual quest. The old Socratic injunction 'Know Thyself' is at the root of the quest of all these three characters—George the narrator, always in love with Catherine, Jerome, who is married to Catherine but is moved by strange longings, Catherine herself, one of the most intelligent and sensitive portrayals of women characters in the whole range of English fiction—all the three are going through a voyage of self-discovery in the novel. 'Who am I really?' is the self-enquiry in which all three engage themselves in the novel. George thinks at the beginning of the novel that 'he had come to terms with myself.' (4) Sally, the daughter of Jerome, is interested in finding out who she really is as she dislikes Jerome hut likes George: "Underneath her banter, she had been disturbed lately and in one way or another she had been asking me questions about the 1930s. I had not realized that her motive had been to lead me on to talk of Jerome. 'Who am I? Whence come I?'" (22) The character in the novel who is most spiritually inclined is Catherine. Indeed, the novel by MacLennan is his 'Portrait of a Lady'—the portrait of Catherine who is an extremely extraordinary lady. Her physical condition of a heart patient, her psychological maturity in the understanding of human strength and weakness, her spiritual strength of selfless acceptance of others—all these are highlighted by the author throughout the novel. To give an illustration:

> Her fate was that rheumatic heart of hers. Her strength, her essence, her mystery in which occasionally I had almost drowned—this I can only call her spirit and I don't use the word in a sentimental sense. Far from it. For to me this has become the ultimate reality, so much so that I think of this story not as one conditioned by character as the dramatists understand it, but by the spirit. A conflict, if you like, between the spirit and the human condition. (25)

Catherine's spiritual maturity, her philosophical outlook and detachment, her utterly selfless appreciation of others, these qualities make her one of the most endearing portraits ever created in English fiction. No wonder George feels, "she was my rock, she was my salvation." (26) Right at the end of the novel, Catherine's face is described in these terms by George: "It had become so transparent one almost felt one looked at a spirit. Light was in it. Light came out of it. Light came from her constantly into me." (371)

This is a remark which sums up the George-Catherine relationship which is the main theme of the novel because she was his 'rock,' his 'salvation.' Instances can be multiplied to emphasize the spiritual dimension of the novel but the third dimension—the philosophical one has been illustrated to emphasize the multi-dimensional approach that can be made to this complex Canadian novel.

V

What has been sought to be indicated in this brief analysis of Hugh MacLennan's *The Watch That Ends the Night* is the fact that it is a great novel which is complex enough and profound enough to be analyzed from a multi-dimensional, inter-disciplinary approach and the three levels of the novel,, the realistic political level, the psychological level, the philosophical level, are all "complementary to each other. In the present cursory analysis, while it is pointed out that at the political level, George is important, at the psychological level, Jerome is important and at the philosophical level, it is Catherine that is important, all these three characters, because of the proverbial *menage a trois* situation and their interaction with each other form an inseparable aspect of the exploration of the human condition. The spiritual, philosophical aspect of the novel is best expressed in the words: "A man must belong to something larger than himself. He must surrender to it." (270) This is reiterated at the end of the novel: "All our lives we had wanted to belong to something larger than ourselves. Whatever the spirit might be, I did not know, but I knew it was there. Life was a gift; I knew that now." (372) The total meaning and achievement of Hugh MacLennan's *The Watch That Ends the Night* can be comprehended only through an inter-disciplinary approach.

The Mystery of Mistry as Tiresias: A Study of "Lend Me Your Light"

> And I Tiresias have foresuffered all.
>
> T.S. Eliot, *The Waste Land*[1]

> But as I slept on my last night in Bombay a searing pain in my eyes woke me up. It was one O' clock. I bathed my eyes and tried to get back to sleep. Half-jokingly, I saw myself as someone out of a Greek tragedy, guilty of the sin of Hubris for seeking emigration out of the land of my birth and paying the price in burnt-out eyes: I, Tiresias, blind and throbbing between two lives, the one in Bombay and the one to come in Toronto.[2]

The present writer would like to argue here that the Tiresias image is meant not only "half-jokingly" but fully seriously. In the same sentence the words "Greek tragedy," "Sin of hubris for seeking emigration" indicate that the metaphor, the image, if you like, is invoked in all seriousness. Were it not so, there was no need to recall it at the end of the tale:

> I mused, I gave way to Whimsy: I Tiresias, throbbing between two lives, humbled by the ambiguities and dichotomies confronting me. (192)

The word 'Whimsy' may be overlooked in the context of being "humbled by the ambiguities and dichotomies confronting me." Here is a 'Confrontation' between the land of birth and the land of adaptation. The present writer would like to suggest that this confrontation is the problem of most expatriate writers and in this case of the nature of Indo-Canadian close encounters but they are of "the third kind"! They are of the third kind because the narrative technique has a third dimension. This is not a simple and straightforward tale told in the first person which might, however simplistically, make one come to the hasty judgement about the "autobiographical element"! And thereby hangs a tale!

The "Mystery" part consists in Mistry making the 'blind' Tiresias to have not only vision or a vision but a double vision. This double vision consists not only in the two lives, "one in Bombay and the one to come in Toronto" but the 'I'-narrator creating another persona for himself, that is, the creation of his brother Percy. The present writer would like to argue that this brother who is the opposite of the third character Jamshed is but his own alter-ego. The 'I'-narrator and Percy are not brothers in the sense of two separate individuals but two aspects of the same person with two separate personalities—in fact, two sides of the same coin. This is the triumph of the narrative technique in this tale of a modern Tiresias who is "throbbing between two lives." In short, the 'I'-narrator and Percy, though they seem to be contradictory are actually complementary to each other. Both of them in a sort of composite personality contradict Jamshed who has no ambiguities, riddles and puzzles to tackle. Perhaps just a few illustrations from this Tale will tell the tale.

II

Right from the word 'Go,' the polarity between the 'I'-narrator and Percy on the one hand and Jamshed on the other is set forth by Mistry—especially with Percy because Percy is mentioned as a great friend and class-mate of Jamshed. It is interesting to see that in spite of Percy's initial admiration for the posh Malabar Hill residence of Jamshed and his Westernization, Percy turns out to be his exact opposite, indeed going to the other extreme and be a patriotic Indian in spite of very difficult and trying circumstances. As far as Jamshed himself is concerned there is absolutely no change in his character and his condemnation of India which started even before he went abroad gets confirmed and hardened after he emigrates to the United States. His initial dislike for India is seen in the passage:

> Jamshed showed a very superficial interest in what little he knew about Percy's activities. Each time they met, he would start with how he was trying his best to get out of the country. "Absolutely no future in this stupid place," he said. "Bloody corruption every where. And you can't buy any of the things you want, don't even get to see a decent English movie. First chance I get, I'm going abroad. Preferably the U.S." (177-78)

This is confirmed in the way he tries to show off when he returns to India from the U.S. on a short visit. He advertises the fact that he is very rich now and he can go to places which ordinary Indians are afraid to go to like the five star Taj Mahal Hotel:

> We were supposed to be impressed by his performance, for we were in an expensive restaurant where only foreign tourists eat on the strength of their U.S. dollars. And here was one of our own, not intimidated within the walls of the five-star Taj Mahal Hotel. In our school-days we could only stand outside and watch the foreigners come and go, wondering what opulent secrets lay inside, what comforts these fair-skinned superior beings enjoyed. Here was one of our own showing us how to handle it all without feeling a trace of inferiority, and now we were ashamed of him. (185)

This sense of being ashamed comes from the open contempt that Jamshed shows in his message from New York:

> Bombay is horrible. Seems dirtier than ever, and the whole trip just made me sick. I had my fill of it in two weeks and was happy to leave. (181)

This lure of the West, what is popularly known in India as "going to phoren" is so widespread that the parents of the I-narrator and Percy, his alter ego, also echo this sentiment:

> My parents announced that I, too, was trying to emigrate, but to Canada, not the U.S. "We will miss him if he gets to go," they told Jamshed, "but for the sake of his own future, he must. There is a lot of opportunity in Toronto. We've seen advertisements in newspapers from England, where Canadian Immigration is encouraging people to go to Canada. Of course, they won't advertise in a country like India—who would want these bloody ghatis to come

> charging into their fine land?—but the office in New Delhi is holding interviews and selecting highly qualified applicants." In the cliches of our speech was reflected the cliche which the idea of emigration had turned into for so many. According to my parents, I would have no difficulty being approved, what with my education, and my Westernized background, and my fluency in the English language. (178)

The love-hate relationship that seems to operate in the case of the I-narrator and Percy perhaps is characteristic of many of the Non Resident Indians (popularly known as NRIs). While on the one hand they don't seem to be able to completely dissociate themselves from their cultural moorings, nevertheless they find the new life quite attractive—attractive enough to emigrate and occasionally pay a visit to the land of their birth, involving not only home thoughts from abroad but abroad thoughts from home! This is another aspect of the Tiresias-like throbbing between two lives, one almost dead and the other powerless to be born. This aspect comes through in the narration of a party of Indians in Canada:

> The truth is, I have been there just once. And on that occasion I fled the place in a very short time, feeling extremely ill at ease and ashamed, wondering why all this did not make me feel homesick or at least a little nostalgic. But Jamshed did not have to know any of it. My letter must have told him that whatever he suffered from, I did not share it. For a long time afterwards I did not hear from him. (182)

This seems to be the Tiresias-like predicament of the I-narrator while his alter-ego Percy seems to have no ambiguity in his attitude which is exactly the opposite of that of Jamshed, who also doesn't have any "compunctious visitings of nature" regarding love of his own country. In fact there is a complete reversal in the attitude of Percy to Jamshed whom he practically held as a model when they were classmates. Percy has started disliking Jamshed to such an extent that he absolutely does not want to even meet him casually when he visits India. Percy is totally involved in his social work at home despite serious drawbacks like attacks on their work. Even then he has absolutely no lure for the West:

> Our work with the farmers started successfully. They got interest-free loans in the form of seed and fertilizer, which we purchased wholesale, and for the first time in years they did not have to borrow from those bloodthirsty money-lenders.
>
> Ever since we got there the money-lenders hated us. They tried to persuade us to leave, saying that what we were doing was wrong because it was upsetting the delicate balance of village life and destroying tradition. We in turn pointed out things like exploitation, usury, inhumanity, and other abominations whose time was now up. We may have sounded like bold knights-errant, but they turned to threats and said it would soon become so unhealthy for us that we would leave quickly enough. (183-84)

Jamshed's bragging about his life in the U.S. leaves Percy cold and he simply wants to get away from his presence:

> When Jamshed concluded his harangue, Percy calmly turned to Mummy and said in his quiet voice, "Could we have dinner right away? I have to meet my friends at eight o'clock. To decide our next move in the village." (192)

Percy's going into the village is the opposite of Jamshed's going to New York. The final predicament of the I-narrator is beautifully brought out at the end of the tale:

> Five days later I was back in Toronto. I unpacked my suitcases, which were quite flat on the return trip and had not required the extra leather straps. I put my things away and displayed in the apartment the little knick-knacks bought in handicraft places and the Cottage Industries store.
>
> Gradually, I discovered I'd brought back with me my entire burden of riddles and puzzles, unsolved. The whole sorry package was there, not lightened at all. The epiphany would have to wait for another time, another trip.
>
> I mused, I gave way to whimsy: I Tiresias, throbbing between two lives, humbled by the ambiguities and dichotomies confronting me. (192)

Let us turn to the beginning of the tale:

> We both left Bombay the same year. Jamshed first, for New York, then I, for Toronto. As immigrants in North America, sharing this common experience should have salvaged something from our acquaintanceship. It went back such a long way, to our school days at St. Xavier's. (173)

After all, it was 'such a long way'—such a long journey. Mistry's interest in T.S. Eliot is seen not only in this tale in using the reference to Tiresias but his use of the expression 'Such a Long Journey'[3] for his novel of that title and used as a motto is taken from Eliot's "The Journey of the Magi":

> A cold coming we had of it,
> Just the worst time of the year
> For a journey, and such a long journey. (68)

At one level the narration seems to be just a straightforward first person narration:

> My days were always full. I attended evening classes at the University of Toronto, desultorily gathering philosophy credits, and worked during the day. I became a member of Zoroastrian Society of Ontario. Hoping to meet people from Bombay, I also went to the Parsi New Year celebrations and dinner. (182)

The well-settled attitude to India and the work ethic of Percy is revealed when he writes about his commitment in the small village:

> Now we're back in Bombay, and Navjeet and I are working on a plan for our return. We've spoken to several reporters, and the work is getting much publicity. We're also collecting fresh donations, so that when we go back we won't fail for lack of funds. (184)

This re-inforces the Tiresias double vision where the I-narrator suffers from a feeling of guilt when he remembers what Percy is doing and what perhaps he himself ought to be doing:

> Having read this far, I put down the letter for a moment. There you were, my brother, waging battles against corruption and evil, while I was watching sitcoms on my rented Granada TV. Or attending dinner parties at Parsi homes to listen to chit-chat about airlines and trinkets. (184)

However, the I-narrator, though throbbing between two lives "one in Bombay and the other one in Toronto," chooses, the life in Toronto.

III

Tiresias is one of the most significant characters in classical myth and legend. The variety of ways in which he has been interpreted is testimony to the fact that many a writer is attracted to using the image for his own purposes. We find an interesting entry about Tiresias in *The Oxford Companion to Classical Literature*:

> Tiresias, in Greek mythology a Theban, who was transformed for a time into a woman for killing the female of a pair of snakes. Zeus and Hera referred to him the question whether man or woman derives more pleasure from love, and when Tiresias supported the opinion of Zeus, Hera struck him with blindness, but Zeus gave him long life and the gift of prophecy. Another story attributes his blindness to his having seen Athena bathing.
>
> In the *Odyssey* Odysseus is sent to Hades to consult Tiresias as to the manner of his returning home. Tiresias also figures in *Antigone* and *Oedipus Tyrannus* of Sophocles, and in *Bacchae* and *Phoenissae* of Euripides. He is the subject of a dramatic monologue by Tennyson in which he recounts the story of his blinding by Athena:
>
> Henceforth be blind, for thou hast seen too much,
> And speak the truth that no man may believe.
>
> Swinburne has a poem 'Tiresias' on the same subject.[4]

For example T.S. Eliot in his *The Waste Land* from which the motto for this essay has already been chosen has two more references to Tiresias:

> I Tiresias, though blind, throbbing between two lives,
> Old man with wrinkled female breasts, can see. . . .
> I Tiresias, old man with wrinkled dugs
> Perceived the scene, and foretold the rest. (68 and 43)

While the reference to Tiresias here is mainly to his being both man and a woman, Eliot makes it clear in his "Notes" that he is more than that and a sort of a spectator-witness to the whole narration:

> Tiresias, although a mere spectator and not indeed a "character," is yet the most important personage in the poem, uniting all the rest. . . . What Tiresias sees, in fact, is the substance of the poem. (52)

The purpose of this little exercise has been merely to take note of Mistry's complex art. "Lend Me Your Light," though it invokes Rabindranath Tagore in its motto from *Gitanjali* and carries the symbolism of light in the tale where the literal dim light of Bombay around Flora Fountain at dusk is linked to the soul-searching question "What would it take, I wondered, to light the lantern of his [Jamshed's] soul?" (190) it justifies the invocation from Tagore "your lights are all lit—then where do you go with your lamp? My house is all dark and lonesome,—lend me your light." (173) In the context of the tale would it be irrelevant if not impertinent to ask the question: "Are we looking for 'light' from the West in modern India?"

Obviously the "India" and the 'West"—as not only Canada is involved but the United States and Europe as well—are not used just geographically but as mindscapes. The story is an introspection, a self-examination, a self-enquiry about one's identity. As the present writer has projected the theory that the two brothers are two aspects of the same 'I,' it is a soul-searching introvert tale with Jamshed the extrovert as the counterpart.

The brief "return of the native" to Bombay only augments his Tiresias-like predicament:

> This trip was not turning out to be anything I'd hoped it would. Jamshed was coming and Percy wasn't. Our parents were disap-

> pointed with Percy, I was disappointed with them, and in a week I would be flying out of Bombay, confused and miserable. (189)

It is true that only one of Mistry's tales, "Lend Me Your Light" in his *Tales from Firozsha Baag*, has been taken up here for comment. In one of his other tales in the same collection called "Swimming Lessons," we get an internal comment about how authors work—especially expatriate writers in the specific context of "throbbing between two lives":

> Mother and Father read the first five stories, and she was very sad after reading some of them, she said he must be so unhappy there, all his stories are about Bombay, he remembers every little thing about his childhood, he is thinking about it all the time even though he is ten thousand miles away, my poor son. I think he misses his home and us and everything he left behind, because if he likes it over there why would he not write stores about that, there must be so many new ideas that his new life could give him.
>
> But Father did not agree with this, he said it did not mean that he was unhappy, all writers worked in the same way, they used their memories and experiences and made stories out of them, changing some things, adding some, imagining some, all writers were very good at remembering details of their lives. (243)

But is not the above analysis of the tale "Lend Me Your Light" a question of mutatis mutandis?—a sample microcosm chosen from the macrocosm?

NOTES

1. Eliot, *The Complete Poems and Plays, 1909-1950* (New York: Harcourt, Brace and World, 1930), p. 44.
2. Rohinton Mistry, "Lend Me Your Light," *Tales from Firozsha Baag* (New Delhi: Rupa, 1993), pp. 173-93.
3. Rohinton Mistry, *Such a Long Journey* (London: Penguin Books in association with Faber and Faber, 1991).
4. *The Oxford Companion to Classical Literature*, ed. Sir Paul Harvey (Oxford: At the Clarendon Press, 1937), pp. 431-32.

Elise Aylen: A Canadian in India
A Classic Case of Cultural Transformation

Elise Aylen was born in Ottawa, Canada in 1904 and she died in Coonoor, India, in 1972. Hers is the case of a cultural transplantation bridging Canada and India. She was the wife of the well-known Canadian poet Duncan Campbell Scott and in her own right was recognized as a literary figure of some note. As R.L. McDougall, who has done extensive research on Elise Aylen including his spending his sabbatical in India tracing her story from Kedarnath to Kanyakumari, at Mysore and Coonoor, points out: "Amongst Canadian writers of the period, it may be said she was in a class by herself."[1] Elise Aylen came from an old Ottawa family and she settled in Coonoor to be the disciple of Swami Yogeswarananda and she has dedicated her remarkable book *The Night of the Lord*[2] to her Guru. The present writer has written separately on this work calling her "A Canadian Pilgrim."[3] However, the present essay is from an entirely different point of view.

The Night of the Lord is Aylen's "Passage to India" which McDougall calls "essentially a spiritual quest . . . her search was beset with problems as old as the history of man: the nature of good and evil; the relation of the real to the unreal, of the spiritual to the material; the nature of the Godhead itself." (134) There is hardly any area in India where she has not stayed—Mussoorie, Agra, Srinagar, Benaras, Delhi, Bombay, Kurukshetra—the legendary battlefield of the *Mahabharata*—Calcutta, Mysore, Pondicherry and Coonoor where she finally settled until her death. Elise Aylen herself is quoted as saying: "I have written a series of poems on the Hindu Gods, which Hindus seem to like very much. They all tell me that I must have had many incarnations in India, and always ask 'However did you come to be born in Canada this time?'"[4] Aylen, before she in Canada this time?'"[4] Aylen, before she finally settled in Coonoor spent some time at Kaser Devi Ashram under the supervision of Lama Anagarika Govinda, a formidable scholar with an international reputation earned through the publication of several books, in particular on Tibetan mysticism. McDougall, who visited all the places associated with Aylen, went to Coonoor and describes his meeting Swami Yogeshwarananda:

> He is tall, probably in his sixties, though he might be more, smooth-shaven, and he has a stock of white hair that falls to his shoulder. He wears a baggy tweed coat that seems incongruous in the hot Indian sunshine, and from beneath the coat the white fold of his Brahman's robes reach almost to his sandals. He has a red kerchief around his neck. Smiling, he raises his arms high above his head. "You have come about Elise!" he calls out. We have not written ahead, and the assumption comes as a surprise. (132)

Elise Aylen's *The Night of the Lord* defies all classification. It can be taken as a novel, as a travelogue or as a spiritual autobiography. At all these levels, though the profound influence of India is seen on this Canadian writer, in the interests of brevity only the third level, namely, the cultural transformation as is seen in this spiritual autobiography, is commented on here. The narration is complex as there are three different 'times' through which the spiritual journey is described. Six chapters out of thirteen take place in 'time present,' five chapters in 'time past' and two in 'legendary time'—taking into account the ancient Pauranik stories, myths and legends of India. In fact, the title 'The Night of the Lord' refers to Shivaratri, the annual worship of Lord Shiva especially during the night after a day's fasting when the vigil is kept throughout the night spent in the contemplation of the Lord. The author herself says that 'This is the story of a journey of which one can see neither the beginning nor the end, but only certain of its resting places.' (1) Thus there is a coalescence of place and time. Some of the 'resting places' are Hardwar, Rameshwaram, Madurai, Srirangam, Chidambaram and Coonoor. Thus it is obvious that the cultural transformation has to do with religious and spiritual life. Indeed it can be described as 'a Canadian pilgrim's progress in India.'[7]

II

The slow but steady cultural transformation that takes place in the life story of a writer is sought to be illustrated with reference to several passages in the text. For example, here is the description of her experience at the temple at Rameshwaram:

> The temple itself was vast, with endless corridors turning and turning as if leading to the heart of a mystery. They drew one deeper, in fold after fold of silence, till the world was remote, unreal forgotten. I felt something change all at once, either within me or without me, as if I had crossed some spiritual barrier, into a profounder silence, into a stilled sanctity. I was near, I was very near, treading on the verge of revelation. (30)

Such an effect is found not only on Elise Aylen but on several visitors from the West. She describes a boy from England:

> He was such an English boy as one might expect to see in the 'quads' of Oxford or Cambridge, carrying a cricket bat or a tennis racket under his arm; not dancing to a flute in a dark South Indian temple, wearing only a blue loin-cloth, and blue ear-rings of lapis lazuli. (34)

Aylen speaks of a group which had arrived from U.K.: 'Reverend Wadsworth, Mrs. H. Dereham, Miss Philippa Dereham, Mr. Angus Dereham' and a little lower down, 'Mr. Miles Barnes' who gave his address simply as 'Delhi.' (38) In fact, Miles can be taken as the British counterpart the Canadian Pilgrim. Much later in the narration we meet Miles again. From Rameshwaram he had gone up to the temple at Kedarnath, a place of pilgrimage high in the snowy mountain, the Himalayas:

> Miles looked older than when I had seen him, very sunburnt and weatherworn. He had put off his western clothes entirely, and wore a loose gerua tunic, reaching to his calves, a cotton shawl folded over his shoulder, and rope-soled sandals. He carried a tall pilgrim

> staff, and had a long rosary of very large beads hung about his neck. (134)

Aylen's understanding of the Gods and Goddesses of India is certainly not superficial. For example, the way she talks about Lord Shiva is revealing:

> Shiva, the most subtle of all the Hindu Gods, of many forms and many names: the Dancer, the Destroyer; the Ascetic; Ardhanarishwara, the Half-Woman-Lord; Kailaspati, Lord of Kailas; Vishwanath, Lord of the World. He is the dancer, self-concentrated, absorbed, rapt in the ecstasy of his own rhythm, yet he is also the Great Ascetic. . . . The symbol here is greater than the word, more subtle, more penetrating. (35-36)

At this point the symbol of Lord Shiva as 'Nataraja' may be explained. The present writer is convinced she knew what she was talking about when she says that 'the symbol here is greater than the word.' Though the dancing Shiva is familiar to the Western collectors of Art pieces, the symbol attached to it is perhaps less familiar. So in the context of cultural transformation, the following explanation may not be irrelevant. Each part and aspect of the dancing Shiva is totally symbolic. The Ganga in the matted hair is a symbol of Holiness and Plenty. The half moon is a symbol of Time and Mind. The circle of flames is a symbol of Perfection, the floating hair is a symbol of Space, the 'Third Eye' a symbol of Jnana—Supreme Knowledge, the right hands symbolize Power of Creation and Sustenance, the two left hands indicate Fire as The Destructive Power as well as symbol of purification. The serpent signifies normal functions in every body, the left hand pointing downwards known as 'Dolahasta' in dance and a left foot pointing upwards in conjunction symbolize the upward thrust of the Jiva—the individual soul, the demon under the right foot symbolizes Mortality, Ignorance and the dark forces, the skin cloth and anklets symbolize valour and inner strength and the face of Nataraja expresses Inner Poise of abiding in the Self—Self with capital 'S' as the symbol of the Absolute and the Transcendental.

Her understanding of the essence of India's spiritual heritage makes her see the essential 'Oneness' behind apparent diversities. Her comprehension of the ultimate oneness of both Shiva and Vishnu is seen in a description of Lord Vishnu:

> In a small cave temple, farther back in the rocky ridges, lay a beautiful Vishnu sleeping on the Serpent of Eternity, that same Ananta, the Endless One that I had seen before at Chidambaram. Beautifully, reposefully the God slept in the vast interval between creation and creation, when life sinks back into stillness and the worlds dissolve. But in the still sleep of the dreamer lies the potential being of all the worlds to come. At last there springs from his navel a lotus, from which those worlds unfold. It is difficult to see how he differs in this sense from Shiva, but if one presses any of these great Hindu Gods far enough, they seem to coalesce in some vast Oneness, great enough to contain all man's concepts of deity. (38-39)

She not only describes a rock-cut at Mahabalipuram showing 'the story of the descent of the Ganges of heaven' (38) but composes a whole poem about river Ganga:

> Holy Ganga, Mother Ganga,
> We pray to thy unceasing waters;
> In thy merciful waters,
> In the flow of thy waters,
> Cleanse me of sin,
> Let my sins be borne away.
>
> Eternal as the snows
> Whence thou comest,
> Eternal as the ocean,
> To which thou goest,
> So are thy waters,
> Thy unresting waters,
> Never failing,
> Our redemption forever.
>
> Holy Ganga, Mother Ganga,
> Bear me at last on thy waters,
> Bear me on thy merciful waters,

Bear me to the endless ocean,
To the unknown depth
Where all life is one. (53)

Such poems—some twenty of them are interspersed in the narration. We learn from R.L. McDougall, an unofficial biographer of Elise Aylen to whom a reference has been made in the beginning of this essay, that in the year she married Duncan Campbell Scott, in 1931, Macmillan published a slim volume of her poems entitled *Roses of Shadow*. He quotes the last poem of the volume called 'Allegory':

One moment—then the leap and the seeking.
Through far things and hidden must my way be cut.
The dull earth severed for a passing.
Through arid reaches and through choking valleys,
By unimaginable courses,
Pressing, faltering
To the sea.

There may I be lost,
Outreaching the limits of being,
The narrow stream
Absorbed in the Infinite.

Thence shall my spirit be drawn forth by the sunlight,
Thence shall I be lifted
To hover in faint cloud-wreaths
Round the brow of the mountain.
In frail spirit caress let me rest there.
From that place whence the waters arose
There shall they return again,
So let me seek my source—
Changeless—
The mountain.[6]

This earlier poem, written twenty years before she came to India has been quoted here to show that coming events cast their shadows before and the poem is prophetic. This desire, 'let me seek my source, 'changeness,' 'The mountain' was fulfilled when she landed in India and stayed till her death. The Himalaya mountains inspired her as much as the temple at Tanjavur, thus unifying the spiritual India as one single unit. All the poems describe her spiritual quest and illustrate her cultural transformation to the extent that she ceased to think of Canada as her 'home.' This unity of India is quietly brought out in her narration of the journey in the North:

> I left Hardwar soon after and did not see the woman again. By a somewhat circuitous route I reached the railhead at Kathgodam, where I took a bus, a small, rickety, mountain bus which made its lively way up the steep passes, by immense gorges and perilous slopes, for some seventy miles along the coiling and ever-ascending road. We stopped halfway at a small village, a cluster of caddies and tea shops. In one of the shops I saw a sadhu sitting, writing hastily in a small note-book. He tore out a sheet and gave it to someone standing by, then returned the note-book to another. As he rose he saw me sitting alone in the front of the bus. All the other passengers had scrambled out to get themselves food and drink. He looked a little surprised, then ordered someone to bring me a cup of tea. 'Take it.' he said to me. 'You have a long way to go.'
>
> There was the ghost of a smile on his lips, and I realized suddenly it was the sadhu I had seen sitting in the niche of the temple at Tanjavur, and mistaken for an image. (88-89)

Thus the Englishman, Miles and this sadhu become living symbols of the spiritual unity of India, connecting Chidambaram and Tanjavur on the one hand and Hardwar on the other. Perhaps the best way to end this account of cultural transformation through transplantation is by quoting a significant poem by Elise Aylen herself:

> O Lord Shiva, thou Compassionate One,
> O Wielder of the trident,
> Whose head is the heaven,
> Whose body is the world,
>
> The Self of all beings,
> To the Half-Woman-Lord,
> Half of whose body is Durga.

Thou Shining One,
O Giver of joy,
To thee I bow down. (58)

NOTES

1. R.L. McDougall, "The Story of Elise Aylen." *Ambivalence: Studies in Canadian Literature*, ed. Om P. Juneja and Chandra Mohan (New Delhi: Allied), pp. 129-48.
2. Elise Aylen, *The Night of the Lord* (Bombay: Bharatiya Vidya Bhavan, 1967).
3. S. Ramaswamy, "Elise Aylen's *The Night of the Lord*: A Canadian Pilgrim's Progress in India," *Ambivalence*. pp. 149-59.
4. McDougall, p. 142.
5. *Ibid.* p. 132.
6. *Ibid.*, pp. 134-35.

The Art of Anne Hebert:
A Study of *Kamouraska*

Tout art, a un certain niveau, devient poesie.

Anne Hebert, "Mystere De La Parole"

Je suis plonge au centre de moi-meme sans remission

Anne Hebert, "Le Torrent"

As a poet, a dramatist, a short story writer and a novelist, Anne Hebert is undoubtedly one of the most important and versatile writers from French Canada. Whether it is her *Les Songes en equilibre* (1942) or *Le Temps Sauvage* (1967) or "Le Torrent" (1950) or *Kamouraska* (1970), one sees the 'unified sensibility' of a great artist and her oeuvre is the result of the exercise of the same artistic consciousness. In each of her works, she has created a unique atmosphere, a special world which represents the authentic French Canada. The thematic links between the various forms of literature in which she has excelled can be demonstrated by a study of her total oeuvre. However, in this short paper what is attempted is to show that the central theme of her *Kamouraska*, an intensely emotional and passionate novel of love, hate and violence is the quest for her authentic self on the part of the protagonist Elizabeth and this scheme is explored purely in poetic terms. It is unmistakably a poet's novel and indeed it can be discussed as 'the novel as poem.' This, in spite of the fact that this novel can be interpreted as a historical novel. As Anne Hebert herself has said on the cover page:

> While this novel is based on an actual event that took many years ago, it is still very much a work of fiction. The real participants in the drama have lent it only their outermost 'official' gestures as it were. From that point on, they have gradually developed within my mind and have come to be imagined creatures all my own.

Arising from this statement it is clear that though it is a novel 'based on an actual event that took place many years ago' it is 'still very much a work of fiction.' The present writer would like to show how this bloody tale of powerful passions is metamorphosed in the mind of the poet to result in a prose narrative that is 'rich and strange.' To use her own expression, how it has 'gradually developed within my mind'—a mind that is essentially the mind of a poet. It is not for nothing that Anne Hebert is recognized as one of the most distinguished poets of French Canada. In her novel *Kamouraska* (trans. Norman Shapiro, Markham-Ontario-Canada: Paperbacks, 1974), Anne Hebert employs to the fullest extent poetic devices like imagery, symbolism and suggestion—*dhvani* as it is called in Indian poetics—rather than direct statement.

It is best to begin with 'the outermost official gestures' of the novel—the matter-of-fact plot-line—before we examine the art by which Anne Hebert transmutes the 'event' into a poetic realization through her creative imagination. The first passage is the indictment against Elizabeth:

> At Her Majesty's Court of King's Bench the jurors for our Lady the Queen, upon their oath, present that Elizabeth Eleonore d'Aulnieres, late of the parish of Kamouraska, in the district of Quebec, wife of one Antoine Tassy, on the fourth day of January in the second year of the reign of our sovereign Lady Victoria, by the grace of God, Queen of the United Kingdom of Great Britain and Ireland, defender of the faith, with force and arms at the parish aforesaid, wilfully, maliciously and unlawfully, did mix deadly poison, to wit one ounce of white arsenic with brandy and the same poison mixed with brandy aforesaid, to wit on the same day and year above mentioned, with force and arms, at the parish aforesaid, in the country aforesaid feloniously, wilfully, maliciously and unlawfully did administer to and cause the same to be taken by, the said Antoine Tassy, then and there being a subject of our Lady the Queen, with intent in so doing feloniously, wilfully and of her malice aforethought to poison, kill, and murder the said Antoine

> Tassy, against the peace of our said Lady the Queen, her crown and dignity. Oyezl (27-28)

As Anne Hebert herself puts it, this is 'the indictment, writ in the Queen's own English, by the masters of this land.' (27) Apart from the sarcasm in the statement, this factual account is to be placed along with a passage right at the beginning where Elizabeth talks about herself:

> Me, Elizabeth d'Aulnieres. Widow of Antoine Tassy, wife of Jerome Rolland. And I felt like laughing in the whole world's face. Oh, what a ride, what a lovely sleigh ride! From Lavaltrie to Montreal. The warrant for my arrest, the two policemen stinking of beer, the ride through Montreal. And in such style! The warden tells me how sorry he is, and he bows and scrapes right down to the floor. The book door shuts behind me. Four moldy walls. The smell of the toilet. The cold. The indictment. . . . Court of King's Bench. Session of September 1840. The Queen against Elizabeth d'Aulnieres-Tassy. . . . My wild youth. Interrogations. Witnesses. And each time I had to spruce up my innocence. . . . Two months locked up, then home. Reasons of health. Family reasons. Good-bye, prison. And good-bye to you, dear warden. You poor bewildered man. Well, you have my maid to console you. Justice can hold her as long as it likes. Two years behind bars. Poor Aurelie Caron. But time wipes the slate. And now you're free, as free as your mistress. A new life, a new start. . . . They will never extradite my lover. Charges withdrawn. (2-3)

This is the epigrammatic statement recollected in agony by Elizabeth right at the beginning of the novel as the 'events' and 'incidents' in the novel are not arranged chronologically and there is no linear 'progression' and there is no 'development' of plot here. Just one more passage to complete the story-line of the novel

> And now my husband is dying once again. Peacefully, in his bed this time. The first time was nothing but violence, blood and snow. Not two separate husbands, one by one, following each other in the marriage registers. But one man, one and the same, rising again from his ashes. One long snake, always the same, coiling himself

> about in endless rings. The eternal man, who takes me and lets me go. Over and over. His first face, cruel. I was sixteen, and I wanted to be happy. Swine! The filthy swine! Antoine Tassy, squire of Kamouraska. Next, love in all its sombre radiance. Eyes, beard, lashes, brows. All black. Black love I'm sick, Doctor Nelson and I'll never see you again. . . . My, what a lovely triptych! The third face, so gentle, so dull. Jerome. (26)

These three passages tell us the 'story' of the novel *Kamouraska*—Elizabeth as a young girl, married to Antoine Tassy, the Squire of Kamouraska, the drunken and cruel womanizer, her unsuccessful attempt to get Tassy murdered by employing her servant to go to Kamouraska and poison her husband, her falling in love with Doctor Nelson from Burlington, U.S.A., who out of love for her murders Tassy and flees to the States and her second marriage with the dull Jerome Rolland. It is as Madame Rolland that she is recollecting the whole story of her life. However, the narrative is so complex and multi-dimensional that this is where we see Anne Hebert's art.

In fact, almost everything in the novel is hinted at and suggested obliquely rather than directly stated. Just as in poetry. In Indian terminology, it is *vakrokti* and not *swabhavokti*. The rich texture of the novel is due to the sheer poetry of the narrative technique which has even dispensed with chapters. It is one continuous narration with a few spaces in between to suggest a shift in time or in mood. The atmosphere of French Canada—of Montreal, Sorel and Kamouraska—is created with deft linguistic strokes. The placid, quiet world of Sorel and the tempestuous life of Tassy at Kamouraska are beautifully contrasted. The name Kamouraska itself:

> Riviere-Ouelle. Cling for dear life to the name of that village. . . . (The village just this side of Kamouraska.) Try to stretch time, make it last. (Five or six miles from Kamouraska.) Draw out the syllables 'ri' and 'vi' as far as they can go. Then let them open out on the 'ere.' Try hard to hold on to the 'Ouelie' But no use. That liquid name, rippling and rolling, runs off like a brooklet through the mossy grass. Soon the green part, jagged sounds of 'Ka-

> mouraska' will jangle against one another. That old Algonquin name. Rushes-beside-the-water. . . . I play with syllables. Hit them hard against one another. To drown out all those human voices that could rise up against me in one great throng. To raise a great roar of syllables loud and harsh. Turn them into a shield of stone. A sling to protect me, tough and resilient. 'Kamouraska! Kamouraska.' (204)

The Quebec landscape, the music of the place-names and the vast expanses of French Canada—they are all evoked with a poet's sensitivity in creating the atmosphere for high drama—poignant tragedy:

> It is clear and mild. No wind at all. Sainte-Anrte-de-Sorel, Saint-Franscois-du-lac, Pierre Ville, Nicolet. (190)

The account of the journey of Elizabeth to Kamouraska is worth quoting in this context:

> A two-week journey. Long deserted roads. Through forests. Little village inns. The fatback and molasses make me sick . . . The heat is unbearable. The rain comes through the hood into the carriage. Louiseville, Saint-Hyacinthe, Saint-Nicolas, Pointe-Levis, Saint-Michel, Montmagoy, Berthier, L'Islet, Saint-Roch-des-Aulnaies, Saint-Jean-Port-Joli. . .
>
> The air of the river, downstream, filling my lungs. The evenings, growing cooler. Stronger and stronger, the smell of the sandy banks.
>
> Riding along, Antoine Tassy points to an invisible line where the river becomes as salty as the ocean. Elizabeth d'Aulnieres lets her thoughts run back home to the sweet fresh waters of the Richelieu.
>
> Saint-Anne, Riviere-Oulle, Kamouraska. (71)

This kind of evocation of the spirit of the place is parallelled in the deft strokes with which Anne Hebert contrasts human characters for example between Antoine Tassy and Doctor Nelson. However, in the interests of brevity only one example of Hebert's superb craftsmanship will be illustrated here—the way she has used the imagery of snow and blood in portraying the murder of Tassy. We have almost to infer what happened and the indirection by which the event is described reveals her superb art.

The whole narration is handled in various stages through a number of witnesses who reveal what they saw bit by bit, stage by stage, the unifying factor being the image of blood and snow. There are seven witness-accounts worked into the narration which describe the journey of Doctor Nelson to kill Tassy and the journey back until he flees to the border and crosses over to the United States. Let us look at just a few passages dealing with the snow/blood imagery:

> Antoine Tassy, the squire of Kamouraska. . . . The squire . . . Antoine . . . of Kamouraska. . . . Dear me, indeed! What an enormous wedding. . . . Oh, what an enormous crime; Elizabeth! Your poor dear husband, dead in the snow! Who could have killed him? In the cove of Kamouraska? The snow. . . . And so much blood. . . . Your pretty face all stained! Snow. . . . Snow. (43)

These disjointed interjections are an exact reaction to the murder by the acquaintances of Elizabeth when they hear the news—the disbelief, the horror of it all. But it is not stated in the novel that it is their reaction. The reader has to infer it. Contrast this with the thoughts of Doctor Nelson who wants to kill him:

> Black on white. Beard, hair, eyes, heart. . . . Oh yes, especially your heart. Black, black, black. . . . The horse and sleigh. And the white snow, blinding, under pounding hooves, all the way to the end of the road. Of every road. Where the horizon teeters on the edge of emptiness. To kill a man, out at the farthest reaches of all that emptiness. To keep from falling over, into the abyss. Just long enough to take aim and fire. A gallon of blood to shed. About a gallon, not much more. You're a doctor. You know about things like that. (188)

This rumination of Nelson which brings in the colour black in short staccato sentences still retains the snow-blood imagery. Not only is the heart of Tassy 'black' but the horse of Nelson is also 'black'—appropriately enough. The fears of Elizabeth regarding the murderous journey of Nelson from her Rue Augusta home in Sorel, the 'sanctuary' which is now hardly safe, is typical:

> What is Doctor Nelson doing down by the mouth of the river? Has he managed yet to. . . . A desert of snow, chaste and sexless as hell itself. No use to scan the limitless white expanse. . . . Has George Nelson lost his way? Has he frozen to death in the snow? . . . Far as the eye can reach, a motionless sea of snow. . . . Yet all of this taking place beyond me. In a far-off land full of blood and snow. (195, 196, 200)
>
> And the snow blowing all around us. (210)
>
> The knowledge of what it must be like to lose your way in the dead of night, in the snow and cold. When you have just killed a man. Lord, who would dare to beg your mercy? The terror, the agony of it all. (210)
>
> The sweat, the panic. . . . The musty stench of blood. (213)

The various witness-accounts of the people who saw Nelson and his sleigh also have the same central imagery of blood and snow. Here is an account of how Nelson tries to bluff his way through as recollected by one of the witnesses—but didn't succeed to fool him:

> "You didn't get all that filthy on our roads around here, did you? Not with this nice white snow!"'
>
> "The last place I stopped, I had to leave my sleigh in their slaughterhouse. That's why all the blood. . . ."
>
> "They sure weren't awfully clean at that inn, to mess up your sleigh like that and get your skins so dirty. At least they could have worked them off. . . ."
>
> "I was in a hurry. (214)
>
> He poured hot water from the kettle while I stood and rubbed. We got rid of the biggest one. But there was so much blood, all dried up and mixed with snow. . .
>
> When I got up it was daylight. I saw blood on the floor, all over. And I said to my hired girl, 'There's no two ways about it, child. That man has killed someone!' She said so too. 'There's no two ways about it. That's the only thing it could be. Just go and look outside the porch, where they threw all the blood.' I went and looked. There was blood on the snow. I was frightened to death and I started to shake all over. When I saw all that mess and all that blood, I said to my husband, 'Clermont, it's pretty plain. That man

> has killed someone. . . . I told him a couple of times that man must have killed someone.' Then I went into the stranger's room to get the basin he washed his hands in. The water was full of blood. . . . I found blood all over the quilt and drops of blood on the floor, around the bed. . . . And I saw those skins of his trimmed around the edges, all red with blood . . . the blood spreading and freezing over the white, white, snow. (217-19)

How effectively Anne Hebert has worked into even a witness-account the central imagery of blood is seen from the above passage.

Since *Karmouraska* is a tale of blood and passion placed on the snowy Kamouraska, the relentlessly oppressive and recurring images of snow and blood are the very warp and woof of this fictional narrative, worked in with a poet's sensitivity. Instances can be multiplied but just two more references must suffice:

> Little Robert is telling how, when he showed up, Monsieur Tassy was already dug out. His bead and his hair were full of blood and snow. . . . They found him buried in the snow and ice. At the edge of the cove at Kamouraska. (228)
>
> "I'm a doctor after all and I swear it's just not human. All that blood in one man's body!" (238)

As was mentioned at the beginning, Anne Hebert creates in all her works a unique atmosphere which represents the authentic French Canada. In *Kamouraska*, the wild, four hundred-mile drive through the Canadian winter down St. Lawrence River with blood on the snow is pictured in such a way that it shows why Anne Hebert is a great writer. The efforts of the central character Elizabeth to find her authentic self through her experiences with Antoine Tassy, Doctor Nelson and her second husband M. Roland in Kamouraska, Sorel and Montreal is delineated by Anne Hebert in her typical poetic approach. The same approach is found in her celebrated short story "Le Torrent" where she describes the life of Francois and his revolt against his mother and where the torrent—the water imagery—becomes the central point of reference. Anne Hebert's themes are the awakening of the senses, the rejection by the outside world and the rejection of the outside world by her characters, resulting in the retirement into an interior world which represents purity and innocence as contrasted with the outside world which represents evil and solitude. These themes result in the silence of the interior life and the actions of her characters become self-oriented. The deafness of Francois in "Le Torrent" is the central symbol characteristically enough. Anne Hebert's use of symbolic language is what establishes the links between the various forms of literature she has mastered. Perhaps it is best to end this essay with one final illustration from Kamouraska:

> Farewell, my love. . . . Your horse and sleigh are taking you off, taking you far, far away, over the hardened snow. . . . I can't see you now. I can't hear you now. Your scent is beginning to vanish from my skin. Just a piece of your clothing. . . . Your jacket, your scarf. . . . And I curl upon it and bury my head. Like a faithful dog. . . . Maybe then, secure and calm, steeped in the scent I love, maybe then I would fall asleep.
>
> When I close my eyes I see you there, prey to the strange mutations of man and beast. One image haunts me more than the rest. You remember that cock in the stable? The one that would climb up on your horse and spend all night on his back? . . . On morning his spurs get tangled in the horse's mane. Your horse rears up. Stands on its hind legs. The cock is struck, spreads his wings out wide. Tries to get loose. Flutters and flaps in wild despair. To no avail. Cock and horse seemed joined together in one incredible monstrous whole. A single creature thrashing about. A single flailing of wings and hooves. A single bedlam of snorts and cackles. Filling the stable with its awful din, beating against the walls of the stall. In one great shower of feathers and hair, one burst of shattered planks and twisted nails. . . .
>
> I scream. That frenzied fury, my love. It's you. That cock and that horse, fused into a single being. It's you. You, gal-loping blithely off. Off on your way to horror and murder. Over a perilous snow-covered road. . . . Farewell, my love. Au revoir, mon amour. We won't be seeing each other again until what must be done is done. Out there, in Kamouraska. (189)

Environmental Changes and Social Values in French Canada: Focus: Montreal

Grand port of navigations, multiple
The Lexicons uncargo'd at your quays,
Sonnant though strange to me; butchiefest, I,
Auditor of your music, cherish the
Joined double-melodied vocabulaire
Where English vocable and roll Ecossic,
Mollified by the parle of French
Bilinguefact your air![1] A.M. Klein, "Montreal"

Hugh MacLennan, in his novel *The Watch that Ends the Night* has written so perceptively about Montreal that the city itself is the main character in the novel along with other human characters. MacLennan writes:

> It is a curious city, Montreal, and in this story I keep returning to the fact that it is. Strangers never understand its inner nature, and immigrant families, even from other parts of Canada, can live here two generations without coming to know it in their bones. I am absolutely certain that Montreal is the subtlest and most intricate city in North America. With her history she could not have been otherwise and survived, for here the French, the Scotch and the English, over two centuries have been divided on issues which ruin nations and civilizations, yet have contrived to live in outward harmony. This is no accident. They understand certain rules in their bones.

It is significant that MacLennan is the author of *Two Solitudes* and in the novel *The Watch*, there are more than two dozen references to Montreal. The narrator introduces himself by saying "My name is George Stewart and I come from what might be called an old Montreal family."[2] Bilingualism is an important aspect of Montreal reality and it has affected environmental and social changes of far-reaching importance:

> Canadian literature may be divided into two parts, somewhat like a tree with two great roots. One root is deeply buried in the culture of France. The other is just as deeply buried in the traditions of England. One part of the Canadian literature is written in French, the other in English. But the branches of this tree are firmly Canadian.[3]

However, Robertson Davies puts it with a difference in a symbolic context:

> Of late years two stereotype figures have arisen from the pressures of our political situation; one is a wistful, large-eyed, pitiful girl in the peasant dress of the eighteenth century, and the other is a coarse-grained, large-footed, evil-visited Scotch banker, to whom she is bound in a hateful marriage from which she seeks to escape.[4]

Davies is lecturing in the United States when he says this and there is an interesting comment on Canada and the United States in Anne Hebert's *Kamouraska*, perhaps the most "Quebecois" novel. Anne Hebert in her own inimitable powerful lyricism depicts the environmental changes—religious, linguistic and social—and how they affect the social values of the characters:

> They're afraid of you, Doctor Nelson. As if, under all that obvious selflessness of yours—too obvious, perhaps—some fearsome identity lies hidden . . . that original flaw, deeper than your Protestant religion, deeper than your English language. . . . Look. Look hard. It's not a sin, Doctor Nelson. Only some terrible grief. . . . And your mother, pressing her face against the window, crying. In Montpelier. In Vermont.
>
> This American independence is readily too much for good loyalists to bear. Isn't it better to pack the children off to Canada? Send them away before this new spirit pollutes and infests them? Let them even become Catholics. Even learn French if they have to. Anything, just so long as they keep their allegiance to the British crown.[5]

In a lighter vein, the crossing into Canada from the United States gives an idea of bilingualism in Quebec in a poem by Wayman:

"Wayman in Quebec"

> It began simply enough, as an invitation
> for Wayman to spend a few days at a lake
> in the Laurentians, but as soon as Wayman's car
> crossed over the bridge at Hull, what's this?
> the trees along the highway suddenly became
> "les arbres" and a house
> "une maison" and Wayman was relieved to see
> the familiar face of Colonel Sanders
> revolving reassuringly, but, wait,
> below his customary goatee, the Colonel was now selling
> "les pullets frits a la Kentucky."
>
> Wayman felt he should be able
> after all those high-school tests he had endured
> to inquire politely as to where he was going:
> "Bonjour. Ou est la direction a Cheneville?"
> Or something like that, but his heart sank
> at the last moment, and all he could stutter out
> was "Cheneville? Cheneville?" Keep going that
> way you are headed
> a calm voice confronted him. Turn left at the
> next set of lights
> all this time Wayman was considering
> How do you say Wayman in Quebec? and also
> What am I doing here?[6]

David Fennario's *Balconville* has been described as the first Canadian bilingual play. Fennario's locale is "the Pointe," the working class district of Pointe St. Charles in Montreal. His characters reflect the social values of a politically disenfranchised urban proletariat doomed to poverty by socio-economic circumstances. *Balconville,* which was first performed at the Centaur Theatre in Montreal on January 2, 1979, is a *coup de theatre*[7] with nearly a third of the dialogue in French. However, it must be noted that

> In Quebec a high percentage of literary artists—poets, singers, playwrights and novelists—want a unilingual independent Quebec.

> . . . However vaguely they take public positions, they have moved in a different way than their fellows in English Canada. They now occupy a different intellectual, cultural, ideological reality than English Canadians do. They have made certain psychological moves. They have undergone a revolution of ideas.[8]

Raymond Brazeau, speaking about the environmental and social changes observes:

> The nineteenth century in the history of the literature of French Canada is at best characterized by the optimistic, idealized and often intangible values of the French left in Canada after the Conquest. The first writers were French-born, French-influenced and French-oriented. It was their duty to maintain the language, the culture and the tradition of France in an Anglo-Saxon/American territory. But more than this it was soon their duty to find a compromise situation for the establishment of a French identity on the North American Continent. This explains why so much of the literature of that period is defiant, overly patriotic and superconscious of its survival.[9]

Hubert Aquin who has been active in legal political activities concerned with the state of *Quebec*, born in Montreal in 1929 has been a writer with one determined focus. He is the author of *Prochain episode* and *Trou de memoire*. As Raymond Brazeau observes:

> His books look forward to a revolution in the province of Quebec, a radical change in the present order that will establish the Quebecois as master in his own house, culturally and economically liberated from the English capitalist influence. His fervour is shared with other Quebec authors of the past ten years namely Paul Chamberland, Claude Jasmin, Pirre Gravel, and especially Pirre Vallieres who have made literary attempts to further the revolutionary cause. (75)

Eugene Benson, in his Foreword to Elaine Nordochio's book *Theatre and Politics in Modern Quebec*, says:

> The Parti Quebecois under Rene Levesque strove to forge a new political conscience for Quebec, as a new generation of writers

(Garneau, Tremblay) rejected the "Francairs de France" in favour of Joual with its connotations of the anti-establishment and the proletariat, and as intellectuals in every field from education to economics changed Quebec into a secularized *society*—The Queen in Gurik's *Hamlet, Prince de Quebec* (1968) is the Catholic Church incestuously bedded with King Claudius or English Canada. Perhaps the most theatrical play illustrating the validity of Dr. Nordochio's theme that theatre and politics in Quebec enjoy, and always enjoyed an enriching symbiotic relationship is Michel Tremblay's *Hosanna* (1973) which is a parable about Quebec and politics. Tremblay is unequivocal on this point:

> My play, *Hosanna* deals in a symbolic way with the problems of Quebec. Although *Hosanna* concerns two homosexuals, one exaggerated masculine character, it is really an allegory about Quebec. In the end they drop their poses and embrace the real identity. The çlimax occurs when Hosanna Kills Elizabeth Taylor and at the end appears naked on stage and says he is a man. He kills all the ghosts around him as Quebec did. We are not French but we are Quebecois living in North America![10]

As Elaine Nordocchio, commenting on the 30s and 40s in Quebec, says:

> The Thirties and the Forties were difficult periods in Quebec's social, political, and economic history. Maurice Duplessis, who held power in Quebec almost without interruption from 1936 to 1959 was a traditionalist and a conservative who sought to make Quebec a closed society, isolated from the rest of the world.[11]
>
> The rapid modernization of Quebec meant that the dramatists from Jacques Languirand to Jean-Claude Germain often created characters who were torn between their desire for personal and collective prosperity and their attachment to more traditional values and modes of behaviour . . .
>
> The family came to represent many of the values associated with the past and a rural way of life. Many writers situated their characters in a rather traditional family setting and then proceeded to criticize the merits of this particular social institution in the context of a modern, urban Quebec. The works of Michel Trem-

> blay for example, stressed the traditional moral values they foster. At the same time, his plays clearly defended the right of the Quebecois to partake of the material advantages of modernization and urbanization.[12]

Like the rest of the Western world, Montreal too was affected by the 30s. In MacLennan's *The Watch that Ends the Night*, the change in political environment due to the Spanish civil war is very effectively out by the fate of the main characters of the novel, of how the society and its values were affected. Jerome's obsession about Spain, Fascism, Franco, Communism etc., forms the very crux of the matter. George, the narrator of the story is himself a commentator for the CBC. The social changes in Montreal after the 30s affect the lives of all the three main characters in MacLennan's novel. As the narrator says: "I tell you, there are few people who passed through the Thirties who even dare or can recall what time was really like or what it did to human beings." (123)

II

Now we can look at two illustrations from the Montreal context—Michel Tremblay's plays and the South Asian—especially Indian Diaspora—in Montreal.

For Michel Tremblay, the Quebec question was very much a linguistic and economic one. Tremblay was the first dramatist not only to write consistently in Joual but also to deal explicitly with the sorry state of Quebec working class.

Michel Tremblay's *The Impromptu of Outremont* can be described as a French-Canadian social document. It is a remarkably powerful play about the changing environment and its effect on social life and values in Quebec and the play discusses the old, traditional bourgeois values in relation to the onset of working class pop culture at various levels—of language or literature, music and the social institution of marriage in Montreal. The "locale" of play is "Outremont" in Montreal and the Westmount society is contrasted with the working class area of East Montreal. Speaking about Michel Tremblay, Elaine Nordocchio says:

> Tremblay's stylized use of working-class French was an immediate subject of debate. Never before had there been a play that had used joual so exclusively and so clearly and aggressively presented life on the wrong side of the tracks in Montreal. (66)

Yvette in *Outremont* says: "If Fernende heard me, she would correct me and I would apologize after having said, 'Pardon, je suis z'en forme' with the laison in the right place. I would assume an air of contrition and put on a face of shameful defeat."[13]

Not only in language but the changing social environment resulting in questioning old values and taking a new direction in marital affairs is depicted in Outremont. Lorraine marries not in her own class but a gardener and goes to live in an Italian Ghetto. As she puts it:

> Guido came into my life like a dagger thrust cleanly into the heart, making a beautiful sound that's clear, frank, precise! Freedom! An open Window! Honesty! . . . I was carried off, like in a cloak and dagger movie, practically out on my bedroom window. My prince charming had an accent to make you shudder and nothing in his hand, but a rake, but God, he was beautiful and I loved him! I almost left Outremont on the seat of a tractor to become what sister Fernande calls common, as she holds her nose, but what I call real laughing, singing and tapping my feet. (58)

If class is one thing that is affected, the other thing that affected Quebec society was the linguistic barrier—more precisely, the crossing of it—Francophone and Anglophone, Serge is the new French Canadian—a no-nonsense angry young man, takes Lucienne to task in Tremblay's *Bonjour la Bonjour*:

> Don't play games with me. You're supposed to be the smart one in the family, the tough one who made it . . . you are telling me you want to drop everything for Robert? Come on! You'd never leave all this to go hole up in a basement with a guy who stinks of paint. I know you better than that. Look, you are married to a doctor, an Anglais on top of that. . . . You've got two lovely teenage twins

> who flatly refuse to learn French because their father speaks nothing but English.[14]

The changed social values and environment is also seen in a sort of generation gap, in their attitude to Colonialism and France. In *Bonjour*, the old man Gabriel, and the young Serge are a contrast. The old man's nostalgic attitude to France is revealed when he says:

> Don't be afraid to tell me about Paris. Oh, I know I've never been there, but I've read a lot. I've read all about that stuff. . . . May be I've never past Guy and Dorchester either, but I've read upon all those things. (13)

But for Serge Paris is just another city. Elsewhere in the play when a character says: "We thought you might come home with a girl from Paris." (11) Another character replies: "Serge has better taste than that." (12) Without multiplying illustrations, it may be recognized that one of the things that has changed is the attitude towards Colonialism. The changed attitude to Colonialism is also represented symbolically in *Bonjour* as seen in the following dialogue.

Lucienne: You can sleep in the guest room. You know it's been refurnished, eh, since you left? I got tired of the Colonial. It looked cheap.
Serge: I'm the one who told you that . . .
Lucienne: We put the Colonial in the basement . . . (28)

The shifting of the 'Colonial' to the 'basement' represents an important change in the French Canadian society.

Finally, in the context of the social changes depending upon the general socio-cultural environment in Montreal, perhaps it is not irrelevant to mention the Indo-Canadian encounter. Uma Parameswaran's new pioneering book[15] introduces us to the South Asian presence—the Indian diaspora in Canada. She sees four phases in the interaction between the environment in Canada and the South Asian Canadians out of which the fourth phase is relevant here. She speaks of their active participation in the larger, political and social arena outside one's own immediate community." (1) One of the plays in the volume, *Saclit Drama*, Rana Bose's *Baba Jacques Dass* and *Turmoil at Cote-Des-Neiges Cemetery* is entirely placed in Montreal. It was staged at the Centaur Theatre, Montreal in 1987. Rana Bose who moved to Montreal in 1977 is a founding member of "Montreal Serai" and has staged nine plays in English. He sees the Serai mandate to be "a willingness to critique contemporary social issues, with a strong Montreal flavour." (174) Binoy, the protagonist of *Baba Jacques Dass* is significantly a writer and is an angry young man. Lack of time prevents an analysis of the play here but in the context of cultural environment and social change only two short passages may be quoted which are comparatively less explosive in language:

Jacques: You have probably evolved an asshole egotist—in conflict with your environment. Was she ever involved in social work in India? (stops) Never! Now she's widow with a mission going around in circles saving the lives of so many women. All of a sudden she has found a new meaning to her life. Was she born with social work on her mind? (204)

In the general Indo-Canadian cultural context, the following dialogue may be interesting. The situation is an "Interview":

Mr. Fraser: What is your date of birth?

Binoy: 15th August 1947, Independence Day.

Mr. Fraser: Good, good. Do you speak Hindu?

Binoy: No, sir, but I do speak Hindi and I can of course speak Bengali, some Urdu, Assamese, Oriya. I also know a few words in Gujarati, Marathi and even some Punjabi . . . but as far as the Southern languages go I am not all that conversant. How many languages do you speak?

Mr. Fraser: (bowled over) Well, I'm English Canadian, eh, so I speak English of course Je parle francais, aussi, mais . . . (excitedly) I can also speak American, yes (suddenly gets angry) but wait a minute. I am asking the questions. You are the one who has made the application to live in Canada. (199)

The social changes that are taking place in Canada and the different cultural environment to which the Indian emigrants have to adopt themselves in their behaviour there is a complex two-way traffic. Thus in sketching the environmental changes and social values in Canada—with particular reference to French Canada, and specifically with Montreal, the scene is as complex as it is interesting.

NOTES

1. Klein, "Montreal," *The Oxford Book of Canadian Verse* (Toronto).
2. Hugh MacLennan, *The Watch that Ends the Night* (1958), p. 3.
3. *The World Book Encyclopaedia*, Vol. III (Field Enterprises Educational Corporation, 1975).
4. Robertson Davies, "The Canada of Myth and Reality," *Canadian Literature in the 70s*, ed. Paul Denham and Mary Jane Edwards (Toronto: Holt, Rinehart and Winston, 1980).
5. Anne Hebert, *Kamouraska*, trans. Norman Shapiro (Ontario: Paper Jacks Markham, 1974), p. 125.
6. *Canadian Literature in the 70s*, p. 176.
7. David Fennario, "Balconville," *Modern Canadian Plays*, ed. Jerry Wasserman (Vancouver: Talon Books, 1986), pp. 275-309.
8. Robin Matthews, *Canadian Literature, Surrender or Revolution*, ed. Gail Dexter (Toronto: Steel Rail Educational Publishing, 1978), p. 157.
9. Raymond Brazeau, *An Outline of Contemporary French Literature* (Forum House, 1972), p. vii.
10. Eugene Benson, "Introduction," *Theatre and Politics in Modern Quebec*, Elaine Nordocchio (The University of Alberta Press, 1986), pp. ix-x.
11. Elaine Nordocchio, *Theatre and Politics in Modern Quebec*, p. 21.
12. *Ibid.*, p. 116.
13. Michel Tremblay, *The Impromptu of Outremont*, trans. John Van Burek (Vancouver: Talon, 1981), p. 11.
14. Michel Tremblay, *Bonjour la Bonjour*, trans. John Van Burek and Bill Glassco (Vancouver: Talon, 1975), p. 25.
15. *Saclit Drama*, ed. Uma Parameswaran (Bangalore: IBH, 1996).

Canadian Prairie Experience and the Global Context

> Prairie literature is no more about the physiognomy of the land than is *Hamlet* about Danish politics. Landscape is setting; it is an element of interest, but it is a secondary feature of the literature itself. It is the metaphor that the artist has used to express himself.
>
> Terry Angus

With reference to various regions of Canada like the Maritime provinces, Quebec, Ontario, Saskatchewan, Alberta and British Columbia, it is possible to talk about 'The Maritime Experience,' 'The West Coast Experience,' 'The Prairie Experience' etc. As Terry Angus has pointed out:

> The Prairies are not simply flat desert wastelands as they are often pictured. Alberta's flat land starts to roll into the foothills, then merges with the mountains. Not even Saskatchewan is entirely flat, and Manitoba is heavily wooded, with thousands of lakes, including the enormous Lake Winnipeg. All three, of course, share vast and rugged northlands, rich in natural resources—a far cry from the desert stereotype.[1]

Some of the characteristics of Prairie literature can be identified as the shift from the rural to the urban, leaving the land for the city, Western alienation, the effect of the great depression etc. The farmer, however, remains the symbol of the Prairies. The literature of the Prairies reflects a positive image of the farmer. An attempt has been made here to briefly outline some characteristics of the Prairie region as reflected in the various forms of literature like poetry, fiction and drama.

II

Perhaps the best way to begin the discussion is by quoting the short poem "Prairie Impression" by Margot Osborn:

The world is a silver penny
Impossibly large
And I am in the middle of it,
A penny reaching from rim to dull grey rim of sky
That curves above my head, a lustreless bowl. There is nothing but the snow and I.
The snow in shadowed hummocks is its superscription
But I cannot read the language nor make out the design.
I am alone in this white desolation. Though I move, it travels with me, Featureless,
And I still remain in the middle. (97)

Yes, the snow is in the midst of all. It is the recurring image with the Prairie wind. Duncan Campbell Scott in his poem "Prairie Wind" asks:

Indolent wind on the prairie
Wind that loiters and passes
What are you trying to whisper
To the dead pale prairie grasses [2]

We hear the wind blowing in a great many Canadian poems and it runs almost like a refrain. For example Anne Marriott in her poem "The Wind Our Enemy" starts the first section with the stanza:

Wind
flattening its gaunt furious self against
the naked siding, knifing in the wounds
of time, pausing to tear aside the last
old scab of paint. (8)

The poem ends as it begins, the last and the tenth section of the poem saying:

God, will it never rain again? What about
those clouds out west? No, that's just dust, as thick
and stiffing now as winter underwear.
No rain, no crop, no feed, no faith, only
wind. (15)

The all-pervasive Prairie wind swishes across in the poem "Prairie Born" by R.J.C. Stead:

> We have heard the night wind howling as we lay alone in bed;
> We have heard the grey goose honking as he journeyed overhead;
> We have smelt the smoke-wraith flying in the hot October wind,
> And have fought the fiery demon that came roaring down behind;
> We have seen the spent snow sifting through the keyhole of the door,
> And the frost-line crawling, crawling, like a snake along the floor;
> We have felt the storm-fiend wrestle with the rafters in his might,
> And the baffled blizzard shrieking through the turmoil of the night. (39)

III

Canadian fiction too pictures the wind and the snow and the vast wilderness. This can be seen described in epic proportions in a Quebec novel *Kamouraska* by Anne Hebert. However, since at present the emphasis is on the Prairie experience, that novel will not be commented on here. It is mentioned here to remind oneself that what applies specifically to a particular region also embodies the whole experience of entire Canada and indeed of any extremely cold region, thus making the Prairie experience a universal one in the global context.

The Prairie experience was felt by children too. Fredelle Bruser Maynard in his *Past Perfect* describes this:

> Though childhood on the Prairies (like childhood anywhere) was not without terrors, it was singularly unhurried. We were not going anywhere, that was clear. Nobody was going anywhere. Farmers' sons came to town on Saturday night for groceries; that was adventure. (43)

He also points out that ecology played a dominant role in the consciousness of the children of the Prairie.

> The Prairie gave me a long childhood, and an instructive one. Though my father did not farm I grew close to the soil, aware of elemental forces. Sun, rain, and the land: those were the ultimate

> realities. Long before the word became fashionable, I was an ecologist, aware of the intricate interdependence of all living things. I breathed the rhythm of the seasons and watched the weather. (44)

This Prairie experience, again is not just regional but global. However, it is rooted in the particular Canadian consciousness. As it has been pointed out earlier, the farmer remains the symbol of the Prairies and hard work is a part of it. Another example of this can be given from the same author.

> Along with hard work, life on the Prairies called for self-sufficiency. It was no accident, I think, that the Canadian readers started us off with the tale of the Little Red Hen. There was just no use expecting other people to help you grind your grain of wheat; they had their own interests to look out for. (45)

Perhaps the most archetypal Prairie writer is Margaret Laurence. In the interests of brevity none of her novels is commented on here but only a short story entitled "The Loons". This is a remarkable condensation of the tragic life of a child narrated by another child. The child Piquette changes during the course even in this short story as in the case of a full fledged novel. From the self-conscious, gawky girl who is slightly physically handicapped, after a couple of years she turns up almost in an unrecognizable manner full of hope and happiness. However, this is short lived and she meets her end too soon in life. The story takes place in the typical Prairie region. The physical topography, the flora and the fauna are accurately described right at the beginning to set the scene for the tragic tale.

> Just below Manawaka, where the Wachakwa River ran brown and noisy over the pebbles, the scrub oak and grey-green willow and chokecherry bushes grew in a dense thicket. In a clearing at the centre of the thicket stood the Tonnerre family's shack. The basis of this dwelling was a small square cabin made of poplar poles and chinked with mud, which had been built by Jules Tonnerre some fifty years before, when he came back from Batoche with a bullet in his thigh, the year that Riel was hung and the voices of the Metis

> entered their long silence. Jules had only intended to stay the winter in the Wachakwa Valley, but the family was still there in the Thirties, when I was a child. (85)

Margaret Laurence with her unerring skill uses the lake birds of the title, the loons, literally as well as metaphorically. The ethnic background of the dwellers is also described. It is mentioned that "The Tonnerres were French half-breeds, and among themselves they spoke a patois that was neither Cree nor French. Their English was broken and full of obscenities." (85) This perception is modified later when we read:

> Unlikely as it may seem, I had only just realized that the Tonnerre family, who I had always heard called half-breeds, were actually Indians, or as near as made no difference. My acquaintance with Indians was not extensive. I did not remember ever having seen a real Indian, and my new awareness that Piquette sprang from the people of Big Bear and Poundmaker, of Tecumseh, of the Iroquois who had eaten Father Brebeuf's heart—all this gave her an instant attraction in my eyes. I was a devoted reader of Pauline Johnson at this age, and sometimes would orate aloud and in an exalted voice, "West Wind, blow from your Prairie nest; Blow from the mountains, blow from the west"—and so on. (89)

IV

Talking of Indians, we move on to Prairie drama where Indians figure and the injustice that was meted out to them by the white man on both sides of the border, the United States as well as Canada. It is presented with astonishing historical precision and fairness. Sharon Pollock in her play *Walsh* gives a touching picture of how the white man broke his word and sent the Indian to his death across the border. The action takes place in the Prairie region. Even the Indian dialect is reproduced in a few places in the play. Pollock who is known for her bold and uncompromising attitude, it may be mentioned here, has also written about Indian Indians (the East Indians as we are called in her play *The Komagata Maru Incident*). However, as this is placed in the far

West, in British Columbia, in Vancouver actually, no further comment is made here.

The other play which is taken up for comment here is a typical Prairie drama and it is very dramatic though just a one-act play. *Still Stands the House* by Gwen Pharis Ringwood is an intense and charged drama of the Warren family consisting of Ruth, Bruce Warren's wife, Hester who is sister of Bruce and Bruce Warren himself. The fourth character is an outsider, a sales agent who wants to negotiate a land deal. Again the farmer and the attachment to land is the central theme. Though this can be construed as a universal phenomenon, the present play particularizes it to such an extent that it is the Prairie itself which is the central character. The atmosphere is defined right in the first stage direction itself.

> The icy wind of a northern blizzard sweeps across the Prairie, lashes about the Old Warren farmhouse, and blows insistently at the door and windows. But the Warren house was built to withstand the menace of the Canadian winter and scornfully suffers the storm to shriek about the chimney corner, to knock at the door and rattle the windows in a wild attempt to force an entrance. (50)

The ubiquitous snow and frost presents an oppressive atmosphere, including a bad blizzard in which both the husband and wife are tragically lost forever at the end of the play. The most powerful character in the play is Hester Warren who is so much attached to the ancestral farmhouse and opposes its being sold for any price. The central conflict is between the wife and the sister. While the wife wants to move out, the sister tries to prevail upon her brother not to sell despite the attraction that is held up by the sales agent. The wife pleads:

> If we go, I'll want this child, Bruce. Don't you see? But I'm not happy here. What kind of a life will our child have? He'll be old before he's out of school. He'll be like this hyacinth that's broken before it bloomed. (68)

Hester doggedly asserts her fierce attachment to the house:

> I stayed home when Mother died and kept house for my little brother and my father. I was very beautiful, they said. My hair fell to my knees, and it was black as a furrow turned in spring. I can have a husband any time I want, but my duty is here with Father. You see how it is. I can't leave him. (72)

In fact though the father is no more physically, it is he who is still the most powerful force in the house. The stage direction makes it clear:

> Above is a portrait of old Martin Warren, who built this house and lived in it until his death. The portrait is of a stern and handsome man in his early fifties, and in the expression of the eyes the artist has caught something of his unconquerable will. (51)

It is this "unconquerable will" that Hester has inherited. She says "This is my house. You can't change it. Father gave it to me. There isn't any room for you. No room." (72) The tragic intensity hits us at the end of the play when we see Ruth the wife going out into the blizzard following her husband to find him as he had gone out with the coal-oil lamp which was not fully filled. When she wants to go out, Hester offers to fill her lamp but deliberately does not do so as she wants her to get lost and die out there in the cold blizzard along with her husband. The stage direction at this point is worth quoting:

> Ruth disappears up the stairs. Hester moves a step toward the lantern, taking off the top of the coal-oil can. She hesitates and looks for a long moment after Ruth. With the strange lucidity of madness, slowly, deliberately, she places the top back again on the can and, moving behind the table, sets it on the floor without filling the lantern. (73)

Thus, though the tragedy is played out in the Prairies, obviously it reaches out to the global level as strong emotions like love and hatred even when it applies to lifeless things like house and the land. This theme is universal. In conclusion as Terry Angus has observed:

The Prairie provinces are heterogeneous as a result of many and varied odysseys, and their literature reflects a cultural mosaic. The prairie experience includes all these diverse experiences, and the result is a variety which defies generalization

In the last analysis, people are people, and any attempt to ascribe a fixed set of unique characteristics to prairie writing would be artificial and false. The people who have written novels, dramas, poems, and prose about the prairies are relating human responses to a particular environment, something all artists do everytime they create. (2)

NOTES

1. Terry Angus, ed., *The Prairie Experience* (Macmillan of Canada. 1975).
2. Duncan Campbell Scott, "Prairie Wind," *An Anthology of Commonwealth Verse*, ed. Margaret J. O'Donnell (London: Blackie), p. 162.

A Note on Canadian Biculturalism

We look
    like a geography but
  just scratch us
and we bleed
        history

Miriam Waddington

Culture, like charity, begins at home. Indisputably culture and language are interlinked. Thus, Canadian bi-culturalism has to be discussed in terms of Canadian bi-lingualism. Canadian bi-culturalism is a fact—a fait accompli. That is why Hugh McLennan talked about 'two cultures.'

> Canadian Literature may be divided into two parts, somewhat like a tree with two great roots. One root is deeply buried in the culture of France. The other is just as deeply buried in the traditions of England. One part of the Canadian literature is written in French, the other in English. But the branches of this tree are firmly Canadian.[1]

As the poet and dramatist, Robertson Davies says in a symbolic context:

> Of late years two stereotype figures have arisen from the pressures of our political situation; one is a wistful, large-eyed, pitiful girl in the peasant dress of the eighteenth century, and the other is a coarse-grained, large-footed, evil-visaged Scotch banker, to whom she is bound in a hateful marriage from which she seeks to escape.[2]

This vision of a demure French girl, representing *la belle France* and the 'coarse-grained, large-footed, evil-visaged' Anglo is represented with similar implications in a play. Some of the questions related to Quebec nationalism that pervaded the Sixties are dealt with in Gurik's *Hamlet, Prince du Quebec* (1968). Elaine F. Nardocchio points out:

> Gurik uses Shakespeare's play as the vehicle for a dramatization of key political events in Quebec history. Gurik's Hamlet (Quebec) tries to be faithful to his father's ghost (France's General de Gaulle). He also spends much of his time reading a book called 'One Hundred Years of Injustice,' wondering aloud whether it is desirable to be or not to be . . . free. Each of Shakespeare's original characters assumes the persona of a real-life participant in Quebec's Quiet Revolution and subsequent events. The Queen is the Church; the King, the English-speaking community; Polonius is Lester Pearson and Ophelia is Jean Le Sage (sic). It is Gerald Pelletier and Jean Mearchand (Rosencrantz and Guildenstern) who betray Hamlet (Quebec) and Pierre Elliot (Laertes) who finally kills the young man.[3]

The Queen in this play is the Catholic Church incestuously bedded with King Claudius or English Canada. The entire play evokes the image of an oppressed country which has been betrayed from within and from without. This realization brought about the rift between the Anglophone and Francophone Canada and the battlecry '*Vive, le Quebec Libre*' was taken up. This antipathy to the English Canada is seen in several places in Quebec writing. For example, in Michel Tremblay's *Bonjour la Bonjour*, the angry young man in the play, Serge, tells off Lucienne:

> Look, you're married to a doctor, an Anglais on top of that, you've got a seventy thousand dollar house in Cartier ville, a charming son who's started to knock up the neighbourhood girls and two lovely teenage twins who flatly refuse to learn French because their father speaks nothing but English.[4]

II

The Canadian bi-culturalism can be discussed under several aspects like colonial, political, social, linguistic and even humour and these categories run through various genres like drama, poetry, fiction and satire.

Colonial consciousness is the common curse of all Commonwealth countries and nostalgia for France is as bad as nostalgia for England. This feeling of nostalgia is exploited and the people of the older generation are held up to ridicule by the no-nonsense youngsters. This is clear in Serge's reaction to the old man who is nostalgic for France.

> Don't be afraid to tell me about Paris. Oh, I know I've never been there, but I've read a lot. I've read all about the stuff. I got the whole map of Paris right here in the old noggin. Your old man is not stupid you know. Maybe I've never been past Guy and Dorchester either, but at least I've read up on these things. You know the Eiffel Tower? I can tell you where it is. It's on the left bank. And Notre Dame, I know where that is too. It's on the Ile de la Cite. Victor Hugo talked so much about that in his book.[5]

This is particularly so because the old man has never been to Paris. Another young person in the same play, Lucienne, uses the word 'colonial' to refer to the old furniture but the same can be applied to anything colonial: "You can sleep in the guest room. You know it's been refurnished, eh, since you left? I got tired of the Colonial. It looked cheap." This nostalgia for France is used by Roberval in George Woodcock's play *The Island of Demons*. As a part of cursing Marguirite in the play, he tries to evoke her sentiment for the old country.

> Lady, do you remember the country of your childhood,
> Those wide French plains swept golden with the wheat
> Breaking against the grey walls of cathedrals,
> The wandering streams, the woods, the evening gathering
> Over the mushroom meadows and the primrose lanes.[6]

The discussion of colonialism naturally leads to the political situation of modern Canada. In this context Hubert Aquin must be remembered. Aquin was born in Montreal in 1929. After studies in Political Science in France and in Switzerland, he returned to Canada where he was successively engaged in various roles in radio and television and wrote the remarkable book *Prochain episode*. After that he wrote *Trou de memoire* in 1968 and

L'Antiphonaire in 1970. He is a political activist and as a writer has one determined focus. His books look forward to a revolution to the province of Quebec, a radical change in the present order that will establish the Quebecois as master of his own house culturally and economically liberated from the English capitalist influence. His enthusiasm and commitment are shared by Quebec authors like Paul Chamberland, Claude Jasmin, Pierre Gravel, and especially Pierre Vallieres who have made literary attempts to further revolutionary cause. The 1960s was a very important period for the emergence of Parti Quebecois. In 1959 Jean Lesage led his Liberals to a sweeping victory in the Quebec provincial election of 1960 with the campaign slogan *il faut que ca change* (Things Must Change). In 1962 he reaffirmed his popularity with a new slogan, more overtly and self-assuredly nationalistic: *Maitres chez nous* (Masters in Our Own House). Since cultural development was becoming increasingly interrelated in Quebec to history, politics, and economics, the government involvement in cultural affairs also increased. In 1960 the Federal Government set up a co-lingual National Theatre School in Montreal with separately administered French and English language sections. At the provincial level the Liberals established a Ministry of Cultural Affairs in 1961. Georges Lapalme was Quebec's first Minister of Cultural Affairs. In 1961 the provincial government created the Office de la langue francaise (French Language Bureau) to look into the state of the language and to begin distributing educational bulletins on the vocabulary used in Quebec. In the early Sixties, the Montreal daily newspaper *Le Devoir* published a series of articles by an anonymous critic who called himself *le Frere Untel* (Brother Anonymous). *Le Frere Untel* (Jean-Paul Desbiens), supported by Andre Laurendeau, the Devoir's editor, denounced the form of the French language spoken and taught in the schools. As an example of the unique character of Quebec's language, he strongly reiterated Laurendeau's claim that the current Quebecois pronunciation of the word for horse was not *cheval* as it was taught, but rather something like *joual*.

The word *joual* soon came to designate the distinctive popular idiom of Quebec, especially of Montreal; a mixture of Anglicisms, Old French, neologisms and standard French. The term had both pejorative and nationalistic connotations. Some felt that *joual* was a black mark to be erased from French-Canadian culture. Others adopted it as a flag of Quebec nationalism, a symbol of the Quebecois cultural identity. Everybody had something to say about it.

In the midst of the quiet reform and self-criticism of the Sixties came militancy in the form of a group of terrorists who felt that only radical action could assure Quebec and the Quebecois of a place in the sun. In 1963, the members of the Front de Liberation du Quebec (The Quebec Liberation Front) claimed responsibility for a series of violent acts including the explosion of bombs in public places. The bombs of the FLQ succeeded in focusing the eyes of the rest of Canada on the social turmoil that was going on in Quebec. "What does Quebec want?" became the English-Canadian rallying cry during that troubled time. In 1967 General de Gaulle's famous *Vive le Quebec libre* drew world attention to Quebec's struggle for independence.

A number of non-violent, political groups and organizations were formed in Quebec in the 1960s to try to deal with the issue. The Parti Quebecois, a provincial political party advocating the independence of Quebec, was founded in 1968. In 1964 the 'Theatre de Quat Sous' began presenting some of Montreal's most interesting and provocative theatre, including several of Michel Tremblay's plays.

As a part of the social scene, Michel Tremblay is of special significance. Aggressively working class from East Montreal, he attacks the upper class from the West Mount and Outremont regions in Montreal. In his play *Impromptu of Outremont* he attacks the four sisters who were all brought up to be sophisticated ladies by their impractical mother and all four sisters are failures in life in four different ways. David Fennario's *Balconville* has been described as the first Canadian bilingual play. Fennario's locale is "the Pointe," the working class district of Pointe St. Charles in Montreal. His characters reflect the social values of a politically disenfranchised urban proletariat doomed to poverty by socio-economic circumstances. *Balconville* which was first performed at the Centaur Theatre in Montreal on January 2, 1979 is a *coup de theatre* with nearly a third of the dialogue in French. At this point it may not be inappropriate to ask with Robin Matthews:

> What is the language of English Canada? How long is it since we thought seriously about that question? Is Canadian language U.S. colloquialism? Is it CBC announcer language? Is it the language of the U.S. 'left'? Is it something else? How does the average union organizer in English Canada speak? What do Canadians expect to hear when they discuss with one another the serious questions of their polity?[7]

English versus French takes on a serious turn and again, Tremblay's revolt is as much against language as about social pretences. In his *Impromptu* he is making fun of the fastidious French used by Fernande who thinks of herself as a custodian of the proper Parisian French in Canada. The struggle between *langue francais* and *joual* assumes quite serious proportions in the discussion of bi-culturalism through bi-lingualism. However, there seems to be a hankering after approval of France in the Francophone Canada. This is perhaps a colonial hangover in spite of the case of protesting the Canadian identity. In Tremblay's play *Outremont* Fernande asks 'What must foreigners think when they hear our lousy French? I don't want the whole world thinking everyone here speaks joual!' As Robin Matthews says:

> In Quebec a high percentage of the literary artists—poets, singers, playwrights and novelists—want a unilingual independent Quebec. . . . However vaguely they take public positions, they have moved in a different way than their fellows in English Canada. They now

> occupy a different intellectual, cultural, ideological reality than English Canadians do. They have made certain psychological moves. They have undergone a revolution of ideas.[8]

It must be conceded at this point that in spite of the antipathy between French and English, a majority of the Canadians speak both the languages with ease and can shift from one language to another wherever they stay in Canada. This bi-linguilism is reflected in a poem like the following:

> Grand port of navigations, multiple
> The Lexicons uncargo'd at your quays,
> Sonnant though strange to me; but chiefest, I,
> Auditor of your music, cherish the
> Joined double-melodied vocabulaire
> Where English vocable and roll Ecossic,
> Mollified by the parle of French
> Bilinguefact your air![9]

In a lighter vein, Irving Layton, in his poem "Anglo-Canadian," comments:

> A native of Kingston, Ont.
> —two grandparents Canadian
> and still living
>
> His complexion florid
> as a maple leaf in late autumn,
> for three years he attended
> Oxford
>
> Now his accent
> makes even Englishmen
> wince, and feel
> unspeakably colonial.[10]

The multi-culturalism of Canada—especially the Anglophone and the Francophone aspects—are seen for example in the short story "The St. Urbain Street Heroes" by Richler:

> Early every Friday morning the French-Canadian farmers arrived with poultry, vegetables, and fruit. They were a skeptical bunch,

> with hard, seamed faces, but the St. Urbain Street wives were more than a match for them and by late afternoon the farmers were drained and grateful to get away. The women, who were ruthless bargainers, spoke a mixture of French, English, and Yiddish with the farmers. "So *fiel, Monsieur*, for dis *kleine* chicken? *Vous* crazy?"[11]

It is perhaps fitting that this discussion should be brought to a close with a facetious, fanciful, humorous and satirical look at Canada which gradually diminishes and ultimately vanishes completely when the big brother, Uncle Sam, swallows it up.

Ten little provinces sitting in a line;
One cried "Non!" and then there were nine.
Nine little provinces made a big state;
One opted out, and then there were eight.
Eight little provinces, God's other heaven;
One said "The hell with it," and then there were seven.
Seven little provinces; mostly in the sticks;
One turned Red and then there were six.
Six little provinces hardly did thrive;
One went back to Britain, and then there were five.
Five little provinces, feeling rather poor;
One struck oil, and then there were four.
Four little provinces clung to the sea;
One let go, and then there were three.
Three little provinces swore to be true;
One joined Jamaica, and then there were two.
Two little provinces, manning their gun;
One pulled the trigger, and then there was one.
One little province, Canada alone;
Uncle Sam inhaled, and then there was none.[12]

NOTES

1. *The World Book Encyclopaedia*, Vol. III (Field Enterprises Educational Corporation, 1975).

2. Robertson Davies, "Canada: Myth and Legend," *Canadian Literature in the 70s*, ed. Paul Denham and Mary Jane Edwards (Toronto: Holt, Rinehart and Winston, 1980), p. 2.
3. Elaine F. Nardocchio, *Theatre and Politics in Modern Quebec* (The University of Alberta Press, 1986), p. 61.
4. Michel Tremblay, *Bonjour la Bonjour*, trans. John Van Burek and Bill Glassco (Vancouver: Talon, 1975), p. 25.
5. *Ibid.* p. 13.
6. George Woodcock, "The Island of Demons," *Two Plays* (Vancouver: Talon Books, 1977), p. 54.
7. Robin Matthews, *Canadian Literature. Surrender or Revolution*, ed. Gail Dexter (Toronto, Canada: Steel Rail Educational Publishing, 1978), pp. 157-58.
8. *Ibid.*, p. 157.
9. Klein, "Montreal," *Oxford Book of Canadian Verse*, ed. A.J.M. Smith (Oxford University Press), p. 260.
10. Irving Layton, "Anglo-Canadian," *Canadian Humour and Satire*, ed. Theresa Ford (Macmillan of Canada, 1976), p. 33.
11. Mordecai Richler, "The St. Urbain Street Heroes," *Canadian Humour and Satire*, p. 68.
12. Eric Nicol, "From Mother (Canada) Goose," *Ibid.*, p. 3.

Immigration and the Indian Diaspora

The Indian immigration into Canada may perhaps be best started historically and chronologically with the *Komagata Maru Incident* as it has been termed. By the early 1900s the Canadian Government believed it had devised an air-tight method to virtually exclude immigration from Asia. In 1914 the 'Komagata Maru' the Japanese steamer entered the Vancouver harbour carrying three hundred and seventy six potential immigrants of East Indian origin. The majority were veterans of the British Army, and all were British subjects. As such they had right of entry to Canada guaranteed by their membership in the British Empire. However, they were forbidden entry by Canadian immigration officials. For the following two months the Komagata Maru lay at anchor. As Sharon Pollock the Canadian dramatist who has written a remarkable 'docu-drama' about the incident entitled *Komagata Maru Incident* points out: "The Komagata Maru returned to India in the fall of 1914, leaving behind only twenty passengers who could prove former residence in Canada."[1]

Most South Asian immigrants came to Canada after 1972. This is an important landmark in the discussion of immigration. However, before we take a look at the process of immigration and the mental adjustment of Indian immigrants into Canada, a word or two about the play *Komagata Maru Incident* itself. It has been described as a brilliantly imaginative and searing portrayal of a shameful and hidden chapter in Canadian history. The play was first produced at the Vancouver Playhouse in January 1976. Sharon Pollock's plays always reveal excellent craftsmanship. She adapts a very interesting mode of presentation in this play by introducing a Master of Ceremonies who plays many roles. She is an exceptional Canadian playwright who has not only written about the Indian Indians, the Sikhs from Punjab who were trying to immigrate into Canada but she is equally concerned with the native Americans, the red-Indians as we call them here. In fact, her play *Walsh* deals precisely with this aspect. A native Indian who innocently believed that they could cross the border into Canada from the United States was totally mistaken and the Canadians proved themselves as untrustworthy as the people of United States. It is a tragic incident which has its echoes in the story of a Sikh. Sharon Pollock is absolutely unsparing in her criticism of White Canadian Immigration policy. Again, she makes the Stage Manager figure in *Walsh*, the Master of Ceremonies say:

> I am telling you my fears—fears that affect each and every Canadian today . . . I fear for my country, and I fear for my people . . . I am not ashamed, nor should you be, to state that this is white man's country! And I can tell you that our British legacy, our traditions, those things that we hold dear, that we have fought and died for, is placed in jeopardy today by a massive influx of coloured foreigners!
>
> The class of East Indian that has invaded British Columbia is commonly known as Sikh. Having been accustomed to the conditions of a tropical clime, he is totally unsuited to this country. . . . The less we speak of his religion, the better. Suffice it to say that unless his ridiculous forms of worship are relinquished, he is an affront to a Christian community. His intelligence is roughly that of our Aborigines. He indeed belongs to a heathen and debased class.[2]

The discrimination against the Asian community is done in a very clever way as the people who were not admitted had a legal right to get into Canada as they were subjects of the British Empire. As the M.C. says:

> In the land of his birth, the average Indian's wage is nine dollars a year. There—you see how we operate, Hopkinson? Never a mention of race, colour, or creed—and yet—we allow British subjects to enter; they are not British subjects; we don't allow them to enter. (11)

This is done in every devious way by imposing a tax to be paid on entry—two hundred dollars per head to be paid before entry. However, a decision was made to allow twenty individuals to enter out of three hundred and seventy six as the people who were permitted to enter according to the immigration officials fulfilled the condition of the legality of their Canadian domicile. The play ends with the stranded people shouting 'Jai Khalsa' a number of times and a character called Mewa Singh is so angry that he fires three times and kills Hopkinson, for which we are told he will be hanged. The play ends with a very touching speech with Mewa Singh on the gallows:

> I am a gentle person, but gentle people must act when injustice engulfs them. Let God judge my actions for He sees the right and the wrong. I offer my neck to the rope as a child opens his arms to his mother. (71)

After the Komagata Maru Incident, the immigration situation in Canada changed. As Robert F. Harney points out:

> In 1947 Prime Minister Mackenzie King called a revival of the mass immigration to Canada that had been curtailed during the depression of World War II. 'The objective of Canada's immigration policy,' he wrote, 'must be to enlarge the population of the country. It would be dangerous for a small population to attempt to hold so great a heritage as ours.'[3]

However, after forty years when Harney is reviewing the situation, he says:

> Today the effects of forty years of mass immigration, tensions between Francophones and Anglophones, the unresolved issue of the rights of the indigenous people, the disruptive pseudo ethnogenesis lurking in the regionalism of the West and the Maritimes, and the traditional fear of absorption by the United States interact to make survival of the Canadian polity a recurring theme in public discourse.[4]

But between the Forties and the Eighties, in spite of the fact that one of the purposes of Canadian Immigration Policy to protect the Pacific Rim from heavy Asian immigration, a large number of Sikhs seem to have emigrated in the late 1960s and early 1970s as Tara Singh Bains points out in his *The Four Quarters of the Night: Life Journey of an Emigrant Sikh*:

> Visitors could come to Canada and apply for permanent residence after they arrived, and it wasn't long before almost every Sikh family had one or more relatives from India staying with them.[5]

1983 marks the eightieth year of South Asian settlement in Canada. Once a small, isolated community in British Columbia, they now number at least 310,000 people.

II

Uma Parameswaran, a leading Indo-Canadian writer and critic, identifies four faces in the personal histories of South Asian Canadians upto 1980s.

> The Phases are: first, wonder and fear at the new world around oneself and nostalgia for the world left behind; second, an overriding impulse to survive in the new world that makes one immerse oneself in one's profession or family, and often precludes political or social participation in the larger society; third, after one has found job security, a turning towards organizational activity within one's own ethnocentric community; and finally, an active participation in the larger political and social arena outside one's own immediate community.[6]

In this brief survey of the history of Indian immigration to Canada, we can notice a different development. In the one-act play by Sadhu Binning entitled *Lesson of a Different Kind*, we take a look at working class newly-immigrated Sikhs who are being exploited by their own community who have settled in Vancouver and have good business establishments. The play shows the Sikh boss exploiting helpless workers. As a female worker says:

> Workers! You call these people here workers? Most of them are boss's family members, relatives or close friends who can't dare say anything against the boss's wishes and then there are people

> like you who are like empty shells just waiting to be thrown away on the garbage heap.[7]

Indeed, she points out that the boss is like any other white employer. Any troublemaker who tries to form the workers' union is immediately dismissed.

There are two centres of theatre activity in Canada by Indians, one at Vancouver called 'Vancouver Sath' and the other at the other end of Canada at Montreal. As Uma Parameswaran points out:

> Montreal and Vancouver are the two major centres of South Asian Canadian theatre but they are quite dissimilar because of their immigration history. . . . The eastern provinces saw an influx of immigrants from South Asia only in the second phase of immigration, 1960s onward. The second phase consisted of highly educated professionals trained in India or in other erstwhile British colonies.[8]

Rana Bose, born in Bengal, educated in the United States who moved to Montreal in 1977 is a Founding member of 'Montreal Serai' and has written and staged nine plays in English. In his *Baba Jacques Dass and Turmoil at Cote-Des-Neiges Cemetery*, he presents a very different picture of Indian immigrants. The protagonist is Binoy and the account of his interview with the Canadian Immigration Officer is hilarious:

Mr. Frazer: What is your date of birth?

Binoy: 15th August 1947, Independence Day.

Mr. Frazer: Good, good, do you speak Hindu?

Binoy: No, sir, but I do speak Hindi and I can of course speak Bengali, some Urdu, Assamese, Oriya. I also know a few words in Gujarati, Marathi and even some Punjabi . . . but as far as the southern languages go I am not all that conversant. How many languages do you speak?

Mr. Frazer: (bowled over) Well, I'm English Canadian, eh, so I speak English. Of course Je parle francais, aussi, mais . . . (excitedly) I can also speak American, yes (suddenly gets angry) but wait a minute. I am asking the questions. You

> are the one who has made the application to live in Canada.[9]

In a manner of speaking, the account of Indian immigration to Canada can be concluded with another quotation from the same play. Rana Bose with his great sense of humour and sarcasm points out that the very Indians who were once denied entry into Canada are now employed in the Ministry of Immigration. A hilarious account of the Indian-born Immigration Officer who is in charge of examining the documents of aspiring Indian immigrants is as follows:

> Ramdas, Shiv Pandey's son, sat behind the glass booth, raking every new arrival with relentless questioning. Ramdas from whom girls would run away giggling, the clumsy son-of-a-bitch who drooled from his mouth every time he opened it was now sitting in the glass booth as Canadian Immigration officer! (176)

Just one last reference to the successful Indian immigrants who think that they have achieved their ultimate goal in life is parodied in the same play:

> Puri: I almost don't feel like . . . you know what I mean. . . . I don't feel like a . . . like an immigrant any longer. . . .
> Soni: What do you feel like?
> Puri: Like a Canadian . . . a natural born Canadian—you know it is a very sacred feeling. . . .
> Soni: Like a sacred cow?
> Puri: A what?
> Soni: A sacred cow.
> Puri: The sacred cow, yes . . . important, accomplished and reliable.
> Soni: An immigrant cow! (223)

What has been attempted here is to focus on the Indian immigration to Canada with reference to historical events as well as how these events are reflected in the creative writing of the Indians in Canada.

NOTES

1. Sharon Pollock, "The Komagata Maru Incident," *Playwrights Canada* (Toronto, 1978). Playwright's note.
2. *Ibid.* p. 26.
3. Rober F. Harney, "'So Great a Heritage as Ours': Immigration and the Survival of the Canadian Polity," *Daedalus. Journal of the American Academy of Arts and Sciences*, Special Number "In Search of Canada," Fall 1988. Issued as Volume 117, Number 4, of the Proceedings of the American Academy of Arts and Sciences.
4. *Ibid.* p. 52.
5. Tara Singh Bains and Hugh Johnston, *The Four Quarters of the Night: The Life Journey of an Emigrant Sikh* (Montreal and Kingston, London, Buffalo: McGill-Queen's University Press, 1995), p. 124.
6. Uma Parameswaran, ed., *Saclit Drama: Plays by South Asian Canadians* (Bangalore: IBH, 1996). Introduction, p. i.
7. Sadhu Binning, "Lesson of a Different Kind," *Saclit Drama: Plays by South Asian Canadians*, p. 90.
8. Uma Parameswaran, *Saclit Drama*, p. vi.
9. *Baba Jacques Dass and Turmoil at Cote-Des-Neiges Cemetery*, *Ibid.* p. 199.

What Price Globalization? Canada and the Quebec question

It has become a commonplace to argue that globalization and localization are Janus-faced aspects of the same process.

Malcolm Waters[1]

Think Global. Act Local

Theodore Levitt[2]

It is a travesty of human civilization that the development of science and technology—nuclear, space and communication—which should have made this globe of ours one extended family *Vasudhaiva kutumbakam* but which has been transformed from the holisticity of a circle into a pyramid with its top, middle and bottom billions. The dichotomized categories of man-woman; West-East, North-South; rich-poor; endowed-disinherited; and dominant-dependent have fragmented humanity itself. And, the irony is, that is all in the name of Globalization.

Women and Globalization[3]

When Shakespeare made Hamlet speak of the 'distracted Globe,' in spite of the obvious pun of referring to 1) Hamlet's own disturbed head, 2) the Globe Theatre of London and 3) The World itself in the present context of globalization, there seems to be little doubt that it is 'distracted.'

The word 'Globalization' has at least three meanings: spherical, total / universal and world-wide. It is the third of these that is relevant here. Although the word 'global' is over 400 years old (OED 1989) the common usage of such words as 'globalization,' 'globalize' and 'globalizing' did not begin until about 1960. In 1961 Webster became the first major dictionary to offer definitions of globalism and globalization. Globalization is the direct consequence of the expansion of European culture across the planet via settlement, colonization and cultural mimesis. Though globalization has been in process for a long time, it has increased its effects and there has been a sudden recent acceleration. Globalization as a recent phenomenon is associated with other social processes like post-industrialization and post-modernization. The term, used mainly in social sciences figured in the writings of Robertson, Turner and Saint-Simon. Globalization is a reduction in the geographical constraints on social arrangements. It is even possible to talk about 'Postglobalization.' In a globalized world the space within which social arrangements are made is a finite but unbounded and seamless surface of the planet.

The idea of the 'Global village' raises certain questions regarding World bodies like APEC (Asia-Pacific Economic Council), EU (European Union), FAO (Food and Agriculture Organization of the United Nations), G8 (Group of Eight Leading Industrial Economies), IATA (International Air Transport Authority), ILO (International Labour Organization), IMF (International Monetary Fund), INGO (International Non-Government Organization), MNC (Multinational Corporation), NATO (North Atlantic Treaty Organization), UNCTAD (United Nations Council for Trade and Development), UNICEF (United Nations International Children's Emergency Fund) WHO (World Health Organization) WTO (World Trade Organization) etc. This seems to undermine the idea of one World with all the different sub-worlds within the one globe. How does one reconcile and integrate the various International bodies into a homogeneous globe? Literally, the Earth was always a globe even when some people thought that it was flat. So in the present Millennium how does one further globalize a globe, emotionally, nationally, theoretically and come up with the idea of oneness in the midst of the myriad many-sided angularities decided by various political, social, anthropological and economic differences? Thus to use the hackneyed expression which has become a cliché 'the unity in diversity' is not quite convincing. Localization is to be taken into account in the context of globalization which seems to be its contrast. We speak of the Third World countries as contrasted with the First World countries. I am not sure what the Second World is. W.H. Auden spoke of 'Secondary Worlds.' Also, the 'developing countries' are spoken of in relation to the 'developed countries.' For my simple mind what 'globalization' has really given is the dot com culture and the menace of the Internet—its use as well as misuse. It has destroyed the sanctity of the privacy and it has also become a means of purveying pornographic material. This despite the fact that it has incalculable and immense advantages. It is commonsense that sitting in any remote village anywhere in the world an individual can get access to all the knowledge necessary and unnecessary if he has the Computer. Surely globalization is here to stay and there is nothing anybody can do about it. It is taking place at various levels of integrating economies, changing the face of families, universalizing ideas of women's equality and it is changing the role of governments. However, it is uneven, fragmented and is still dominated by the West. Unfortunately, at another level it has contributed to the rise of fundamentalism as evidenced in a global terrorist organization like the Al-Queida. Again, for my innocent simplistic mind however much of globalization there is, localization is a fact to consider.

Globalization is a concern more than a concept. Since it has changed the very concepts of nations, and their peoples, it has given rise to certain counter currents which like local / regional movements, cultural and social concerns and values and challenge to the concept of nation itself, ethnically and touches upon human rights issues. The identities through language and race, all get reoriented and the Quebec question is at the very centre of all these issues. Therefore, the present topic has been selected which makes a reference not only to literature but to socio-political issues.

Arguments for and against Globalization can be equally valid. 'The struggle, therefore, is to look for methods of integrating theory and practice without ever simplifying complex-life patterns, especially those ushered in by Globalization.' Manu Chakravarty in 'Conflating Demography and Theory: Emerging Trends in Feminist Studies' says:

> No Theoretician or activist can fail to notice the hybridity let loose by Globalization wherein modern/ primitive, east/ west, rational/ irrational, regional/ national/ global lose all their individual identities and merge to form a homogeneous whole. . . . The idea of a Global village is but an idea that conceals the layers of domination that are a part of its essential core. The advocates of Globalization, especially in areas of capital movement would do well to be aware of the implications of their position. . . . It cannot be construed that only economic issues need to be borne in mind while dealing with the lurking dangers of Globalization. . . . Historians, literary theorists, sociologists, anthropologists, cultural theorists too can become accomplices, unwittingly at times, of the Globalizing forces.[4]

There is also another alternative to globalization which has been termed 'Humanist Project' by Samir Amin who says: 'I maintained that globalization via the market, is a reactionary utopia. We must counter it by developing an alternative humanistic project of globalization consistent with a socialist perspective.'[5] At this point the present writer would like to bring in the spiritual dimension of globalization by referring to certain Indian scholars.

People like Swami Ranganathananda, Dhammananda, Vamadeva Shastri, Dr. Karan Singh, P. Parameswaran and C. Subramaniam have expressed their own views about globalization. While Dhammananda talks of 'The Buddhist response to globalization' and Vamadeva Shastri talks of 'The Hindu response to globalization,' Swami Ranganathananda in his comprehensive view talks about 'True globalization.'[6] Dr. Karan Singh, in a characteristic manner, says: "The emergence of the global society, impelled by science and technology, demands a new holistic paradigm that stresses convergence in place of conflict, complementarity in place of competition, compassion in place of cruelty and a global ethic that would link the deepest insights of science and religion."[7]

P. Parameswaran who is the President, Vivekananda Rock Memorial at Kanya Kumari and chief editor of *Yuva Bharathi* in his essay '*Vasudhaiva kutumbakam,* not Globalization' says:

> Globalization and *Vasudhaiva kutumbakam* are often used as synonyms. But they are not. They denote two basically different attitudes and approacнes. Globalization is the outcome of scientific and technological advancement. It has facilitated an industrial civilization and a flourishing world trade and commerce. It is in its nature materialistic and consumeristic. Its motivating force is self-interest and its success depends upon exploitation of man, nations and nature. There is very little ethical or moral consideration in its working. Naturally it is bound to lead to struggle, competition, rivalry, tension and ultimate destruction. *Vasudhaiva kutumbakam* is essentially a cultural and spiritual concept. It looks upon the whole world as one's own family. Love and harmony, co-operation and mutual support are the basic ingredients here, as in a family. Naturally the idea of exploitation is alien. Individual and collective interests are complimentary to each other. Unlimited consumerism is ruled out because, if every one has to be provided with the necessities, it automatically follows that no one can get away with a disproportionately large share.[8]

II

Now, after dealing with the theory of globalization, it's application to literature with special reference to Canada—(*En poesie Quebecoise* and *Le nationalisme canadien-francais*) the Quebec question can be taken up for the sake of illustration to comment on localization as opposed to globalization involving the concept of Nationalism and Internationalism. It is well-known that global problems have given rise to local problems for which solutions are hard to find. The phenomenon of particularism and nationalism coincides in a remarkable regionalism flourishing in Quebec. This is discussed in terms of the theory followed by responses and reactions to this on the part of the creative writers of Quebec. To refer to 'French Canada' is not enough to discuss the 'Quebec Separatist Question'—Quebec as a nation by itself. The characteristic literature of Quebec was only recognized in the early 20th century. The first writers were French-born, French-influenced and French-oriented. For example, Hubert Aquin who was born in Montreal in 1929 is a writer with one determined focus; his books look forward to a revolution in the province of Quebec, a radical change in the present order that will establish the Quebecois as master in his own house—*Maitres chez nous*, culturally and economically liberated from the English-capitalist influence. His fervour is shared by other Quebec authors of the last ten years namely Paul Chamberland, Claude Jasmin, Pierre Gravel and especially Pierre Vallieres who have made literary attempts to further the revolutionary cause. First, a brief historical / political perspective.

One sees a similar process of liberation in Quebec as the *Parti Quebecois* under Rene Levesque strove to forge a new political conscience for Quebec, as a new generation of writers (Garneau, Tremblay) rejected the 'Francais de France' in favour of *joual* with its connotations of the anti-establishment and the proletariat, and as intellectuals in every field from education to economics changed Quebec into a secularized society. In 1837 a group of *Canadiens* known first as *Les Fils de la liberte* (Sons of Liberty) and later as *Les Patriotes* rebelled against British rule in a struggle for independence that was parallelled in Upper Canada by the efforts of the Reformers, led by William Lyon MacKenzie. There were several sporadic battles in 1837 and again in 1838, but only a few of these skirmishes were won by the *Patriotes* who were badly organized and poorly armed. When the Rebellion was finally put down, most of its leaders had either been imprisoned, exiled, or hanged. The defeat appeared most decisive. In England, Lord Melbourne's government decided to launch an inquiry into the uprisings and engaged John George, Earl of Durham, to lead the investigation. Durham arrived in Quebec on May 29, 1838, and on January 31, 1839 he filed his 'Report and Dispatches of the Earl of Durham, Her Majesty's High Commissioner and Governor-General of British North America.' According to Durham, the crisis in Lower Canada had arisen because of a struggle between the French and the

English. In his view, the troubles went beyond simple political quarrels, and he concluded that the only way to prevent further conflict was to assimilate the French as quickly as possible. He therefore strongly recommended the union of the two Canadas with the aim of creating an English-speaking majority. The French Canadians were crushed. Not only did Durham seem to have no understanding whatsoever of the causes of the Rebellion, he openly supported assimilation through union. Since they had just suffered defeat at the hands of British, there seemed no other means to ensure their survival as a race than to retreat to rural areas and to increase vigilance over their language, culture, and religion. It is not surprising that the English-dominated theatre became less and less popular with the *Canadiens*. In one of Montreal's theatres, for instance, just before the first shots of the Rebellion were fired, a young member of *Les Fils de la Liberte* refused to take off his hat when 'God Save the Queen' was played. A fight ensued that resulted in some broken chairs and bloody noses.

We will take a brief look at how this is reflected in Quebec literature in Canada. Jean Barbeau, Michel Tremblay, Antonine Maillet, and Michel Garneau are only some of the many well-known French language playwrights whose works were read, performed, published and translated. Following Maurice Dupleis' death in 1959 Jean Lesage led his Liberals to a sweeping victory in the Quebec provincial election of 1960 with the campaign slogan *il faut que ca change* (Things Must Change). In 1962 Lesage re-affirmed his popularity by winning another mandate with a new slogan, this one more overtly and self-assuredly nationalistic: *Maitres chez nous* (Masters in Our Own House).

In 1963 the members of the *Front de Liberation du Quebec* (The Quebec Liberation Front) claimed responsibility for a series of violent acts including the explosion of bombs in public places. The bombs of the FLQ succeeded in focusing the eyes of the rest of Canada on the social turmoil that was going on in Quebec. 'What does Quebec want?' became the English-Canadian rallying cry during that troubled time. In 1967 General de Gaulle's famous *Vive le Quebec libre* drew world attention to Quebec's struggle for independence.

A number of nonviolent, political groups and organizations were formed in Quebec in the 1960s to try to deal with the issue. *The Parti Quebecois*, a provincial political party advocating the independence of Quebec, was founded in 1968 by Rene Levesque, a brilliant former minister in the Lesage Cabinet. The PQ sought to obtain by democratic means what the FLQ had fought for with violence; the economic, political, and cultural sovereignty of Quebec.

Nationalism had as many definitions in Quebec during the Sixties as there were political organizations. Nevertheless, during this period it became a strong political force which united the French-speaking population of the province so much so that the appellation *Quebecois* no longer denoted only a resident of Quebec City. The term now designated the whole population of the province of Quebec, replacing the more general, less nationalistic 'French Canadian.'

Since cultural development was becoming increasingly interrelated in Quebec to history, politics, and economics, it is not surprising that government involvement in cultural affairs also increased. In 1960, the federal government set up a co-lingual National Theatre School in Montreal, with separately administered French and English language sections. According to Minville, the defining characteristics of the French Canadian nation are 1) its Christian heritage, 2) family orientation, 3) commitment to liberty and ability of individuals to make their own way in the world, 4) a sense of 'quality' in literature and the arts, 5) belief in tradition and continuity.

Some of the literary representations of the Quebec Separatist Movement are:

1. A symbolic representation presented by Robertson Davies where he speaks of 'a hateful marriage' between Francophone and Anglophone Canada.

> Of late years two stereotype figures have arisen from the pressures of our political situation; one is a wistful, large-eyed,

pitiful girl in the peasant dress of the eighteenth century, and the other is a coarse-grained, large-footed, evil-visaged Scotch banker, to whom she is bound in a hateful marriage from which she seeks to escape. The mismated pair are, of course, Quebec, La Belle Province, and the other part of Canada. A queer song-and-dance team they are.[9]

2. *Le Jeune Latour* (Young Latour), French-Canada's first historical play, dramatizes the political and military confrontation between the French and the English and its effect on two members of the same family. Theatre, at least in this case, compensates for reality, for the young Latour successfully resists the attacks of the English and finally, magnanimously, agrees to shelter his father. What joy there was in the hall that night in 1844 when the French triumphed over the English, if only on stage![10]
3. Robert Gurik's *Hamlet, Prince du Quebec* (1968) deals with some of the questions related to Quebec nationalism that pervaded the Sixties. Gurik uses Shakespeare's play as the vehicle for a dramatization of key political events in Quebec history. Gurik's Hamlet (Quebec) tries to be faithful to his father's ghost (France's General de Gaulle). He also spends much of his time reading a book called *One Hundred Years of Injustice*, wondering aloud whether it is desirable to be or not to be . . . free. Each of Shakespeare's original characters assumes the persona of a real-life participant in Quebec's Quiet Revolution and subsequent events. The Queen is the Church; the King, the English-speaking community; Polonius is Lester Pearson and Ophelia is Jean Le Sage. It is Gerald Pelletier and Jean Marchand (Rosencrantz and Guildenstern) who betray Hamlet (Quebec) and Pierre Elliot Trudeau (Laertes) who finally kills the young man. The entire play evokes the image of an oppressed country which has been betrayed from within and from without. (*Ibid.*, 61)
4. Francoise Loranger's *Le Chemin du roy* (1968) is a rollicking political satire that recreates the climate of excitement and collective euphoria inspired by General de Gaulle's

memorable visit to Quebec in 1967. This is a patriotic comedy in which men and women from Canadian public life meet in a hockey rink to play out the aftermath of de Gaulle's visit. (*Ibid.*, 64) In keeping with the concept of politics as a hockey game, Rene Levesque's 'goal' is independence. His team successfully makes a mockery of Ottawa's policy and the blundering place for unity by politicians like John Diefenbaker, Lester Pearson and Jean Marchand. Throughout the play, the 'arenas' loudspeakers keep the spectator informed of de Gaulle's procession from Quebec City to Montreal ('*le chemin du roy*') culminating in the famous '*Vive le Quebec libre*' speech from the balcony of Montreal's City Hall. Setting the action in a hockey rink, a place that is so closely linked in Quebec culture, was not only a clever device (actually suggested by Montreal's Paul Buissonneau), but also an effective way of bringing home to the Quebecois audience the concrete, cultural dimensions of the federalist-separatist political 'game' that was taking place between Ottawa and Quebec. (*Ibid.*, 64)

5. Loranger's next play, *Medium Saignant* (1970) also developed the idea of participatory theatre, and used the same device of presenting social and political concerns through the microcosm of a particular community. The action of *Medium Saignant* takes place at a town council meeting at which one pragmatic member proposes that a policy of English unilingualism be adopted. He argues that since this development is inevitable, a stop should be put immediately to the expensive practice of printing everything in two languages. It should be noted that *Medium Saignant* was first presented oniy a few months after Bill 63 had been passed in the provincial legislature allowing all Quebecois to send their children to public English-language schools if they so desired. Many critics of the bill claimed that if parents, especially immigrants, were allowed to educate their children in English, it was just a matter of time before Quebec would be overwhelmingly English-speaking. (*Ibid.*, 65)

The contribution of Journals dealing with the Quebec question is not insignificant. For example, *Quebec Studies* published by The American Council for Quebec Studies (ACQS) publishes very authentic studies on all aspects of Quebec. Sometimes a special issue is devoted to one particular area. For example, 'Quebec in the Continental Economy.' The book reviews in ACQS are most helpful in keeping a scholar's knowledge of Quebec upto date. One comes across many talented newer critics like Anthony Purdy (on Hubert Aquin), Raija Koski (on Claire Martin), and Dominique Lafon (on Michel Tremblay). The younger Quebecoise writers include Francine Noel, Monique LaRue, Robert Lalonde and Jacques Marchand.[15] Very interesting point of view are presented about well-known writers and their works. For example, Anne Hebert's *Heloise*, an orphic novel with strong comic gothic aspects, is the only one of Hebert's novels which takes place entirely in Paris, a city where the author has been living and writing for over thirty years. The juxtaposition of these orphic, gothic and Parisian elements lend the novel an autorepresentational but strongly parodic touch. Denise Rochat feels that Hebert's *Heloise* is one literary creation which playfully reverses the Orpheus myth and attempts to give back to Eurydice a central though ambiguous role in the myth of creation. (*Ibid*., 135)

Another interesting article to study would be 'Media Coverage of the 1992 Referendum in Quebec.' On October 26, 1992, Quebeckers and citizens across Canada were asked to vote on a proposed package of constitutional reforms known as the Charlottetown Accord, an agreement intended to draw Quebec more closely into the Canadian confederation. The package also included provisions regarding aboriginal self-government, Senate and Supreme Court reform, and a rearrangement of federal jurisdiction over certain policies. (*Ibid*., 17)

One can state that society remains trapped in a space precisely because the global, indeed finite and because the existential link to space is the inescapable body. Even in a globalized world, our home is the planet. Computers can already simulate a virtual space out of information. This 'Cyber space' bears no relationship to physical space and is limited only by the power of the Computer one uses. In fact, now there is a joke that the next World Conference in whatever subject will be held not in Montreal or Mysore but in Cyberspace that is no place.

Lewis Carroll, one of my favourite authors, in his characteristic apparently innocent but profound manner writes a poem which throws light on Globalization in a lighter vein:

> He had bought a large map representing the sea,
> Without the least vestige of land:
> And the crew were much pleased when they found it to be
> A map they could all understand.
>
> 'What's the good of Mercator's North Poles and Equators,
> Tropics, Zones, and Meridian Lines?'
> So the Bellman would cry: and the crew would reply.
> 'They are merely conventional signs!'
>
> 'Other maps are such shapes, with their islands and capes!
> But we've got our brave Captain to thank'
> (So the crew would protest) 'that he's bought us the best—
> A perfect and absolute blank!'

NOTES

1. Malcolm Waters, *Globalization* (London and New York: Routledge, 1995), p. xii. Most of the details regarding the term 'Globalization' and its range and significance is taken from this book.
2. T. Levitt, "The Globalization of Markets," *Harvard Business Review*, 1983, pp. 92-102.
3. Pam Rajput and Hem Lata Swarup, *Women and Globalization: Reflections, Options and Strategies* (New Delhi: Ashish, 1994), Preface, p. vii.
4. Manu Chakravarty, *Conflating Demography and Theory: Emerging Trends in Feminist Studies* (Department of Women's Studies, NMKRV College for Women, Bangalore, 2001), pp. 11-12.

5. Samir Amin, *Capitalism in the Age of Globalization: The Management of Contemporary Society* (Delhi: Madhyam, 1997), p. 5.
6. Refer to *Globalization* (A Vedanta Kesari Presentation, Sri Ramakrishna Math, Chennai, 2000).
7. *Ibid.*, p. 214.
8. *Ibid.*, pp. 233-234.
9. Robertson Davies, 'The Canada of Myth and Reality,' *Canadian Literature in the 70s*, ed. Paul Denham and Mary Jane Edwards. (Toronto: Holt, Rinehart and Winston), p. 2.
10. Most of the information given here about the political and the social aspects of Quebec is taken from Elaine F. Nardocchio, *Theatre and Politics in Modern Quebec* (The University of Alberta Press, 1986).
11. *Quebec Studies*, A Publication of the American Council for Quebec Studies, Vol. 16, Spring / Summer 1993, p. 132.

Bibliography

Brazeau, Raymond J. *An Outline of Contemporary French Canadian Literature*. Forum House, 1972.

Friedman, J. "Being in the World: Globalization and Localization," M. Featherstone, ed. *Global Culture*. London: Sage, 1990.

McLuhan, M. *Understanding Media*. London: Routledge, 1964.

McLuhan, M. and Q. Fiore. *The Medium is the Message*. London: Allen Lane. 1967.

McLuhan, M. and Q. Fiore. *War and Peace in the Global Village*. New York: Bantam, 1968.

Rickett, Olla Goewey. *The French-Speaking Theatre of Montreal*. Ann Arbor. University Microfilms, 1964.

Rioux, Marcel. *La Question du Quebec*. Editions Seghers. Paris. 1971. Trans. James Boake as *Quebec in Question*, James Lorrier, 1978.

Rioux, Marcel and Yves Martin, ed. *French-Canadian Society*, Vol. I, Toronto: McClelland and Stewart, 1971.

Robertson R. *Globalization*. London: Sage, 1992.

Tougas, Gerald, *Historie de la literature canadienne-francaise*. Paris: Presses Universitaires de France, 1964.

Turner, B. "The Two Faces of Sociology: Global or National?" *Global Culture*, ed. M. Featherstone. London: Sage, 1990.

Twentieth Century Canadian Humour and Satire: A Retrospect

How would you react if someone accused you of not having a good throwing arm, or a mathematical mind, or soulful brown eyes? In all probability, you would shrug your shoulders and retort, "So what?" But if someone were to accuse you of not having a sense of humour, you would quite likely become intensely indignant and consider that you had been seriously insulted![1]

Perhaps the best way to introduce Canadian Humour and Satire is with a poem by Eric Nicol entitled "From Mother (Canada) Goose" where Canada itself as a country vanishes!

Ten little provinces sitting in a line;
One cried "Non!" and then there were nine.
Nine little provinces made a big state;
One opted out, and then there were eight.
Eight little provinces, God's other heaven;
One said "The hell with it," and then there were seven.
Seven little provinces, mostly in the sticks;
One turned Red and then there were six.
Six little provinces hardly did thrive;
One went back to Britain, and then there were five.
Five little provinces, feeling rather poor;
One struck oil, and then there were four.
Four little provinces clung to the sea;
One let go, and then there were three.
Three little provinces swore to be true;
One joined Jamaica, and then there were two.
Two little provinces, manning their gun;
One pulled the trigger, and then there was one.
One little province, Canada alone;
Uncle Sam inhaled, and then there was none. (3)

To continue the geographical, physical, topographical level of Canada, speaking of the various areas and provinces, an Anonymous poem explores the scene further. From the contemplation of Canada as a geographical entity in a comment on the colonial context, Irving Layton's poem "Anglo-Canadian" comments on an interesting Canadian.

> A native of Kingston, Ont.
> —two grandparents Canadian
> and still living
>
> His complexion florid
> as a maple leaf in late autumn,
> for three years he attended
> Oxford
>
> Now his accent
> makes even Englishmen
> wince, and feel
> unspeakably colonial. (33)

While this takes a satirical look at the colonial—specifically British—accent, the affectation notwithstanding in speech, the native Canadian comes through in the telling comparison, his florid complexion compared to "a maple leaf" evoking the Canadian flag! However, the authentic Canadian language including the dialectal variations reflected in the change in spelling indicating the pronunciation is also held up for amusement. For example in "The Road to a Woman's Heart" by T.C. Haliburton only a few lines at random are quoted.

> How on airth do you manage to keep your fruit that's so exposed, when no one else can't do it nohow? (4)

Along with the quaint use of language there is also a Puckish humour.

> "Any man," he replied, "that understands horses has a pretty considerable fair knowledge of women, for they are just alike in temper, and require the very identical same treatment. Encourage the

timid ones, be gentle and steady with the fractious, but lather the sulky ones like blazes.

The female heart, as far as my experience goes, is just like a new India rubber shoe; you may pull and pull at it, till it stretches out a yard long, and then let go, and it will fly right back to its old shape. Their hearts are made of stout leather, I tell you." (7)

II

Not all Canadian humour obviously is directed against women and by all accounts Canadians are not anti-feminist or unchivalrous. In this context one of the less known pieces by a well-known Canadian writer, Margaret Atwood, can be discussed here. Characteristically enough the story is entitled "Rape Fantasies."

It is chosen because it is meant here to represent Canadian humour. "Rape Fantasies" takes a look at 'female space' from a very unusual angle. A traumatic subject is dealt with in a dramatic but light-hearted tone. The story is an ironic contemplation with wit, sarcasm, genial humour and even an element of parody. The would-be rapists—there are eight of them—turn out to be not only harmless but downright pathetic creatures, one or two of them such romantic and chivalrous gentlemen who need to be reminded of their intentions! The first of them is a 'Tarzan' figure who is quite an acrobat who specializes in hanging about skyscrapers from the outside and getting in through the balconies; the second one wants to play it by the book; the third one is a polite gentleman who is very obliging and even opens the top of the 'plastic lemon,' so that then she can 'squirt him in the eye'! The fourth one is a pathetic fellow, short, ugly and 'absolutely covered in pimples.' The narrator says: "I feel sorry for him, in my rape fantasies. I always end up feeling sorry for the guy, I mean there has to be something 'wrong' with them, if it was Clint Eastwood it'd be different but worse luck it never is." (112) The fifth man who jumps in through the window has a terrible cold and so has the girl: "So I ask him why doesn't he let me fix him a Neo-Citran and scotch, that's what I always take, you still have the cold but you don't feel it, so I do and we end up watching the Late Show together." (113) The sixth one gets 'confused' and 'climbs out of the coal chute again, which is how he got in the first place.' (114) The seventh man is a Kung-Fu expert but "I just go ZAP with my fingers into his eyes and that's it, he falls over, or I flip him against a wall or something." (114) The eighth man when he encounters his would-be victim, she tells him that she has leukemia and the doctors have given her only a few months to live. It turns out that he has leukemia himself and has only a few months to live and that's why he wants to be a rapist.

The encounter has a happy ending; not the usual fairy-tale ending 'They lived happily ever after' but simply they lived happily for a while. This is where the parody element comes in:

> So we walk along gently under the street lights, it's spring and sort of misty and we end up going for coffee, we're happy we've found the only other person in the world who can understand what we're going through, it's almost like fate and after a while we just sort of look at each other and our hands touch and he comes back with me and moves into my apartment and we spend our last months together before we die. (115)

This is a nice variation on the proverbial 'love at first sight.' This is love at last sight!—and thus the fantasy ends. Needless to say Margaret Atwood, through her superb mastery of technique, has triumphed at looking at 'female space'—the woman's fantasy world with her own comic genius. As it is pointed out:

> "Rape Fantasies" seems to be a slight work, yet it illustrates some characteristics of Atwood's fiction. The tone is comic, with an edge of satire—in this case at the expense of male views of women's sexuality—and an undertone of gothic sorrow. The ambiguous ending and her ability to engage our interest and sympathy in an essentially vacuous main character also contribute to the short story's success. (117)

In the minds of many people Canadian humour is inextricably interlinked with the name of Stephen Leacock. Just one of his pieces "How I Succeeded in My Business"[3] is commented on here. In this story we move to a very contemporary situation—the world of big business in the modern metropolitan world and the importance of being a success—a winner and to come out a number one man in the rat race. This time the story is not a straight narration but the author's satirical intent and the comments are there unmistakably. "Success"—as the world understands it—is the measure of man but how it is achieved, the technique of achieving the sweet smell of success is hilariously depicted by Leacock: "I had been employed in one business and another quite a good few years, more years than I cared to look back upon; and yet I hadn't made good. I hadn't made good and I knew I hadn't made good and sometimes the knowledge that I hadn't made good made me feel bad." (159) When he sees a tear fall from the eye of his wife he would "go out sit in the backyard and feel real bad." (159) But on one of these moping sessions, wisdom and self-knowledge suddenly dawn upon him and he jumps out of it a happy and energetic man with all the get up and go, push, pull, drive, incentive etc. The discovery consisted of his realizing that he "didn't react upon himself." (160) For the uninitiated reader who doesn't quite understand the brave new technical language and what exactly is meant by "reacting upon oneself," the changed behaviour of Jim Dudley, explains it. The "I" of the story—provides the answer. His wife is the first person to know that he is a "changed man." He breaks with the old-fashioned breakfast that he used to have and orders his wife to fetch him some "farraginous food." He overwhelms her with his veritable harangue on what constitutes a good breakfast: "Don't you realize that bacon contains more units of nitrogen than I can absorb in the office? The attempt to absorb nitrogenous food depresses the nerve centres and lowers the tone of the system. Get me some sour butter-milk and half a dipper of baked beans, so cooked as to emphasize their albuminous properties." (160) The sudden flash of self-knowledge resulting in believing in himself, the newly realized surfeit of self-confidence makes him a bundle of energy. He is ten minutes early for work and the General Manager notices that Jim is a changed man. He treats the General Manager with the same nonchalance with which he treated his wife and puts one over him by pronouncing a series of platitudes. "I'd rather be early than not: the employee who values his employer's time more than his own reacts backward to his own emolument." (161) "The employee who is not hard at it is defrauding both himself and his employer of his proper integument." (161) The General Manager is terribly impressed and he invites Jim promptly for lunch and gives him a very important assignment to "swing a big proposition." (162) There is no stopping Jim now that he has started. He eats his spinach, "cultivated my memory and reacted all the time on everything I saw," (162) including of course Mr. Smith, his customer. Jim doesn't take "No" for an answer, persists in pursuing Mr. Smith, takes him "to a swell restaurant where they had the best spinach" and impresses Smith with his sales talk. He tells him plainly, "You're a big man and this is a big thing: we want to put over something pretty big and you are the man we want on it. You're big." (163) Mr. Smith is naturally impressed and recognizes readily that Jim has "personality" and "that is the biggest thing in business today." (163) Thus it is that Jim "swings many big things" and he lists the top. He becomes head of the company. Right at the end of this success story comes the punch line where Jim's wife asks him what the company makes and sells and he replies: "Don't ask me. I've been so busy swinging propositions and living things up and breaking and eating spinach, that I've never had time to find out what on earth the company does do." (164) Thus it is that Stephen Leacock makes his devastating comment on the brave new business language and the technique of salesmanship.

III

The multi-culturalism of Canada—especially the Anglophone and the Francophone aspects—are seen for example in the short story "The St. Urbain Street Heroes" by Mordecai Richler:

> Early every Friday morning the French-Canadian farmers arrived with poultry, vegetables, and fruit. They were a skeptical bunch, with hard, seamed faces, but the St. Urbain Street wives were more than a match for them and by late afternoon the farmers were drained and grateful to get away. The women, who were ruthless bargainers, spoke a mixture of French, English, and Yiddish with the farmers. "*So fiel, Monsieur, for dis kleine chicken? Vous* crazy?" (68)

After referring to the Canadian land and the people it is interesting to take a look at the notorious cold weather of Canada.

> Our first winter in the settlement,
> the old man said,
> January was so cold
> the flames in the lamps froze.
> The womenfolk picked them like strawberries
> and gave them to the children to eat.
>
> That's the only time
> I was ever a fire-eater. (98)

From this imagist pearl of a poem entitled "Munchausen in Alberta" by Elizabeth Brewster, we move to a longish poem which reads like a ballad. The poem entitled "The Cremation of Sam Mcgee" by Robert Service says the last word on Canadian cold and only just a few stanzas are quoted here to illustrate an extreme form of facetious and sarcastic satirical picture where the humour takes off in a departure from logic.

> There are strange things done in the midnight sun
> By the men who moil for gold;
> The Arctic trails have their secret tales
> That would make your blood run cold;
> The Northern lights have seen queer sights;
> But the queerest they ever did see
> Was that night on the marge of Lake Lebarge
> I cremated Sam McGee.
>
> Now Sam McGee was from Tennessee, where the cotton blooms and blows.

Why he left his home in the South to roam round the Pole God only knows.
He was always cold, but the land of gold seemed to hold him like a spell;
Though he'd often say in his homely way that he'd "sooner live in hell." . . .

Well, he seemed so low that I couldn't say no; then he says with a sort of moan;
"It's the cursed cold, and it's got right hold till I'm chilled clean through to the bone.
Yet 'taint being dead, it's my awful dread of the icy grave that pains;
So I want you to swear that, foul or fair, you'll cremate my last remains." . . .
He crouched on the sleigh, and he raved all day of his home in Tennessee;
And before nightfall a corpse was all that was left of Sam McGee.

Some planks I tore from the cabin floor, and I lit the boiler fire;
Some coal I found that was lying around, and I heaped the fuel higher;
The flames just soared, and the furnace roared—such a blaze you seldom see;
And I burrowed a hole in the glowing coal, and I stuffed in Sam McGee. . . .

I do not know how long in the snow I wrestled with grisly fear;
But the stars came out and they danced about ere again I ventured near;
I was sick with dread, but I bravely said: "I'll just take a peep inside.
I guess he's cooked, and it's time I looked," . . . then the door I opened wide—
And there sat Sam, looking cool and calm, in the heart of the furnace roar;
And he wore a smile you could see a mile, and he said: "Please close that door.
It's fine in here, but I greatly fear you'll let in the cold and storm.

> Since I left Plumtree, down in Tennessee, it's the first time I've been warm." (20-23)

IV

Lest the genre of drama should go entirely unrepresented in this brief survey, only one short play entitled *Shakespeare Revises a Play* by Pierre Berton will be mentioned here. Reworkings, parodies, sequels to Shakespeare's plays in the comic context are a legion. It would be out of place here to make any further comment about this as the present writer has commented on these extensively elsewhere. Specifically in the Canadian context the play *Goodnight Desdemona (Good Morning Juliet)* by Ann-Marie MacDonald[4] converts two of Shakespeare's great tragedies—*Othello* and *Romeo and Juliet*—into hilarious comedies. However, the present play under consideration is a sort of "Deconstruction" of *Hamlet* with a difference! It may be called a subversive and satirical imaginary conversation about *Hamlet*:

> The scene takes place in the Globe Theatre, London. circa 1602. A production meeting is in session. Present are the Executive Producer, the Producer, the Director, the Assistant Director, the Script Editor, two beautiful and leggy Script Assistants, an Agency Rep, a Public Relations man and playwright, W. Shakespeare.

The conversation between Shakespeare and the Executive Producer is particularly funny. The Executive Producer tells Shakespeare:

> Now, look, Shakespeare: this is a commercial enterprise and you better not forget it. I'm getting just a bit tired of your posing about art. I, for one, don't intend to toss two years' investment down the drain just to humour your soul. I pay you to write commercial plays and if you don't like it there are plenty of others around who do. I had Jonson and Fletcher both in my office this morning. So you better blow with the combo, baby, or it's Outsville for you. (117-18)

The great fun of reading this play naturally depends on a good knowledge of *Hamlet* in the original. The so-called "revisions" that are suggested in the light of which Shakespeare has to revise his play are all an integral part of the play that we know. However, we have to only imagine the version of *Hamlet* that Shakespeare had written before submitting it to the production meeting. The humour of the piece partly consists of the kind of commercial and slang expressions which are in vogue in the commercial theatre today. There is no place here to go into details but only some of the "expert suggestions" can be mentioned here. The first suggestion is that a ghost should be introduced. The reason given is "we helped salvage *Julius Caesar* with a ghost scene." (115) The second suggestion is "have old Polonius tell his kid to be thrifty, never borrow money, that sort of stuff." (115) The third suggestion is that Claudius must be murdered "by pouring poison in his ear! It's never been done before." (116) The fourth suggestion is that "There's the teen angle to consider" and "Ophelia ought to be a teenager." (116) Even the psychoanalytical interpretation of Ernest Jones regarding the famous "Oedipus Complex" is hilariously brought in. The Executive Producer suggests:

> Well, the play is awfully short on sex, Will. Oh, now I know what you're going to say! You're an artist! Okay—okay. We respect that, Will, and believe me nobody here wants to interfere with the basic honesty of this play. But couldn't you just suggest a couple of things—like maybe the Prince is secretly in love with his mother. That's always been sure-fire. He could get jealous thinking about her in bed with the guy who knocked off his old man. Just the odd innuendo, Will—in good taste, of course. (116-17)

The fifth suggestion is about the ending of the play. "We've simply got to hypo the ending . . . we got to give them a blood bath. . . . Yeah! Daggers, swords, a cup of poison, maybe! The works! Corpses everywhere!" (117) It is also suggested "have the Prince leap into a grave at one point and dig up an old skull or something." (117) At the end of the play, Shakespeare is made to say:

> All right. I know when I'm licked. Ten more years and I'm going to retire from this hackwork to a place in Stratford where I can hold up my head in society. (118)

This brief discussion of this "Deconstruction" of *Hamlet* once again shows how the material which would have degenerated into a cheap blood and thunder piece is elevated to the level of a great play—the greatest play in English according to the present writer—by the genius of Shakespeare.

V

It has been said that jokes are particular but humour is universal. Canadian humour, in addition to its own authentic touch, enjoys universality as has been seen in the illustrations that have been chosen here. Just one more specific illustration, the poem "Flight One" by Gwendolyn MacEwen should suffice here:

> Good afternoon ladies and gentlemen
> This your Captain speaking.
> We are flying at an unknown altitude
> And an incalculable speed.
> The temperature outside is beyond words.
>
> If you look out your windows you will see
> Many ruined cities and enduring seas
> But if you wish to sleep please close the blinds.
>
> My navigator has been ill for many years
> And we are on Automatic Pilot; regrettably
> I cannot foresee our ultimate destination.
>
> Have a pleasant trip.
> You may smoke, you may drink, you may dance
> You may die.
> We may even land one day. (76)

Humour can be said to arise out of three main ingredients—situation, character and language. We have found all these three ingredients in the pieces selected here for comment.

It is best to end this brief survey in the words of Stephen Leacock himself when he sums up the art of humorous writing, its function and importance.

> No doubt the story-telling habit owes much to the fact that ordinary people, quite unconsciously, rate humour very low. I mean, they under-estimate the difficulty of 'making humour.' It would never occur to them that the thing is hard, meritorious and dignified. The world's humour, in its best and greatest sense, is perhaps the highest product of our civilization. One thinks here not of the mere spasmodic effects of the comic artist . . . but of the really great humour which once or twice in a generation at best illuminates and elevates our literature. It is no longer dependent upon a mere trick and quibble of words, or the odd and meaningless incongruities in things that strike us as "funny." Its basis lies in the deeper contrasts offered by life itself.[5]

NOTES

1. Theresa Ford, ed., *Canadian Humour and Satire* (Macmillan of Canada, 1976), Introduction, p. 1.
2. Margaret Atwood, "Rape Fantasies," *Canadian Literature in the 70s*, ed. Paul Denham and Mary Jane Edwards. (Toronto: Holt, Rinehart and Winston, 1980).
3. Stephen Leacock. "How I Succeeded in my Business," *Famous British Short Stories*, pp. 159-64. The discussion of Margaret Atwood's "Rape Fantasies" and Stephen Leacock's "How I Succeeded in Business" is drawn from a separate paper by the present author.
4. Ann-Marie MacDonald, *Goodnight Desdemona: Good Morning Juliet* (Toronto: Coach House Press, 1990).
5. Stephen Leacock, "Humour as I see It," *Laugh with Leacock*, (Bombay: Jaico, 1957), pp. 287-88.